Nadia Lesy

Robert Anasi

The Last Bohemia

Robert Anasi is the author of *The Gloves: A Boxing Chronicle* (North Point Press, 2002). His work has appeared in many publications, including *The New York Times*, *The Times Literary Supplement*, *The Virginia Quarterly Review*, *The New York Observer*, *Salon* and *Publishers Weekly*. He teaches literary journalism at the University of California, Irvine, where he is a Schaeffer and Chancellor's Club fellow. He is also a founding editor of the literary journal *Entasis*.

The Last Bohemia

The Last Bohemia
Scenes from the Life of
Williamsburg, Brooklyn
Robert Anasi

Farrar, Straus and Giroux   New York

For my mother and father

Farrar, Straus and Giroux
18 West 18th Street, New York 10011

Distributed in Canada by D&M Publishers, Inc.
Printed in the United States of America
First edition, 2012

Library of Congress Cataloging-in-Publication Data
Anasi, Robert, 1966–
    The last bohemia : scenes from the life of Williamsburg, Brooklyn / Robert
Anasi. — 1st ed.
        p.   cm.
    ISBN 978-0-374-53331-1 (alk. paper)
    1. Williamsburg (New York, N.Y.)—Description and travel.   2. Anasi,
Robert, 1966—Travel—New York (State)—New York.   3. Williamsburg
(New York, N.Y.)—Social life and customs.   4. Williamsburg (New York,
N.Y.)—Social conditions.   5. City and town life—New York (State)—
New York.   6. Bohemianism—New York (State)—New York.   7. Social
change—New York (State)—New York.   8. New York (N.Y.)—Description
and travel.   9. New York (N.Y.)—Social life and customs.   10. New York
(N.Y.)—Social conditions.   I. Title.

F129.W75A53 2012
974.7'23—dc23   2011051267

Designed by Jonathan D. Lippincott

www.fsgbooks.com

10 9 8 7 6 5 4 3 2 1

The names and identifying characteristics of some individuals depicted in
this book have been changed to protect their privacy, and all dialogue is
reconstructed according to the best of the author's recollections.

Bohemias. Alternative subcultures. They were a crucial aspect of industrial civilization in the two previous centuries. They were where industrial civilization went to dream. A sort of unconscious R&D, exploring alternate societal strategies. Each one would have a dress code, characteristic forms of artistic expression, a substance or substances of choice, and a set of sexual values at odds with those of the culture at large. And they did, frequently, have locales with which they became associated. But they became extinct . . . Authentic subcultures require backwaters, and time . . .

—William Gibson, *All Tomorrow's Parties*

Contents

The Last Bohemia

Prologue
Summer of 2011

Friday, August 12, 2011

Sonic Youth is headlining a show at East River State Park, a three-block span of waterfront on the Northside of Williamsburg, Brooklyn. It's the latest in a concert series that started back in June and stretched through a July heat wave that broke almost nine thousand temperature records across America, 'causing pavements to explode, railroad rails to buckle, and insects to invade homes in search of shelter and water.' So far, August has been blissfully temperate and a mellow breeze sidles in from the river. The gates opened at 5:30 and two and a half hours later the first distorted guitar riff and drum thuds bring a delighted bellow from the crowd. Since I don't have a ticket, I'm stuck outside.

I've donned a hipster disguise for the occasion: black-and-white shell-toe Adidas, red Toughskins jeans, a black T-shirt from a strip club, large mirrored sunglasses and two death's-head earrings. The Adidas are replicas of shoes Run-DMC rapped about in 'My Adidas,' and part of a breakdancer's uniform—the shell toes help with spins. The Toughskins date to the late 1970s and have a subtle light blue weave that gives them the afterimage shimmer of complementary colors. They're a sentimental choice: I wore Toughskins as a boy in the seventies. The T-shirt, from a strip club further east in Williamsburg, reads 'Pumps exotic dancing.' In a white circle above the lettering, the silhouettes of two naked women revolve around a stripper pole. Their figures are cartoon preposterous. The back of the T-shirt reads 'There goes the neighborhood, BROOKLYN, New York,' along with the address and phone number (718-599-2474, FYI). I've been to Pumps, but I'm wearing the T-shirt ironically, because of course an English PhD couldn't wear it any other way. The sunglasses are Rocawear, Jay-Z's brand. The death's-head earrings are the kind of thing a seventeen-year-old metal head from Fontana would wear. So that's funny. It's an outfit designed to make me conspicuously inconspicuous in American's coolest zip code. Williamsburg was my home for fourteen years but I left in 2008 and everything I see reminds me that it's not home anymore.

Five minutes outside the concert are enough for me to realize that I picked the wrong disguise. Today it's an older crowd for, let's face it, an older band (like, AARP card old). The women wear various takes on sundresses or blouse-skirt ensembles. Most of the guys wear logo'd T-shirts, relaxed-fit jeans and sneakers—American men dressing like American boys. Waistlines and hairlines show that they're closer to forty than thirty. Three decades have passed since Sonic Youth launched from the Lower East Side postpunk scene. I was seventeen when I first saw them in my hometown of Providence. They'd just started touring *Bad Moon Rising* and I'd fake ID'd my way in to join fifty other people in a concrete bunker called the Living Room. I spent the entire show leaning against a pillar as tuneful dissonance tore a hole in the space-time continuum, defeaning and clear, the gateway to something new. Tonight in some small club out in Bushwick or Bed-Stuy a nervous teenager is getting his head blown apart by a sound that will alter American music. But that teenager is definitely not here.

Outside the fence the sound is mud, the vocals muffled. An aging fan rushes by me, dragging a woman and talking in a rush, trying to infect her with his passion. His free hand waves the air in time to the drum rumble. I recognize the intro to 'Death Valley '69' and catch the enthusiasm myself, swept up in a thrill of music I love played live in a new location, the Manhattan skyline a perfect backdrop, sunset seething purple, orange and violet.

But it is not really a new location for me, and my ennui stems from its usual source—the gap between what was and what is. This is not the waterfront as I remember it, as I still want it to be. I take a walk around the park and run into barriers no matter where I go. Pine green plastic sheets hang from the fences. The sheeting has a .org address for an 'Open Space Alliance.' Semicircles have been cut out of the plastic at regular intervals to keep the sheets from flying loose in the wind. An ancillary effect is that you can see inside—see the crowd and the big sound stage, the concert speakers and construction trailers. Of course fans are taking advantage, knees bent, peering through. But it's still a fence and the price of a Sunday in the park is thirty-five dollars, if you bought a ticket before they sold out.

I wind up sitting on a crumbling wall next to the fence on the last block of North Seventh before it hits water. Pavement has replaced cobblestone there, cobblestones and trash.

The L subway rumbles right under my feet and at the end of the block there's a ventilation unit for the subway tunnel. It looks like what it is—the world's biggest floor fan. Orange security barriers block the road a couple dozen yards up from the squat ventilation structure, the barriers manned by men wearing yellow polo shirts and black pants. Lettering on the shirts reads 'Event 565 Staff.' Opposite the park is the far end of the Edge, a complex of condo towers that went up over the last five years on the site of a 'waste transfer station.' Something approaching fifteen hundred units pack the insta-city of colored glass and steel. On a few of the blue-railed balconies, residents peer down at the ruckus.

I leave the wall and walk to Kent Street. Cop uniforms stand out in the swirl of bodies, walkie-talkies crackling. I almost get run over by a bicycle—'It's a *two-way* bike lane,' the cyclist sighs—as I watch touts trying to sell tickets even this late in the game. They don't seem very concerned about the cops and the sour honey of marijuana bastes the air. Toward the park entrance I pass the one building within the park boundaries—an old brick warehouse. Fifteen years ago the span between North Sixth and Ninth held seven warehouses and factories. All the buildings were occupied, but only the squatters in this one warehouse managed to navigate the labyrinth of New York City housing law and gain title. Most of the other squatters were vagrants, drug addicts and prostitutes in need of a place to hide their shame. From luxury boxes, the proud new homeowners watched the other buildings on the lot fired and demolished.

The ground floor of the warehouse semaphores a stint as a restaurant or café, furled black-and-yellow patio umbrellas with the Żyweic logo and heavy iron furniture lining one wall behind yet another fence. The cheap row of mailboxes in the lobby heartens me—at least some early neighborhood settlers managed to hold out. Security and more barriers block the park entrance.

Bags open, the guards say. Ladies have your bag open. No food and drink. Have your tickets out.

As per usual, security is mostly black and Latino, heavy men who pump a lot of iron and eat a lot of pizza. They can't be loving the uniforms—in black and yellow they look like bumblebees and even XXL adheres to man-boobs like spray-paint. Across the river, window lights flash in the dark mass of the cityscape. I've had enough of the new Williamsburg and head off to meet a friend.

Beth and I get socially lubricated at an enoteca on the corner of North Seventh and Wythe. The enoteca encapsulates the contradictions of Williamsburg: outside you have a flimsy three-story house with faux-wood shingles, inside, Sardinia. It's been at least six years since Beth and I have been on the Northside together. Back then she worked for a sports book, boxed competitively and was an occasional stripper. We drank at Black Betty. We drank at Rosemary's Greenpoint Tavern (which isn't actually in Greenpoint). Now she's a writer whose first book is about to be released as a Hollywood feature film. She's given up boxing for yoga but still looks great in her cutoffs.

Out on the street the show is over and we struggle upstream through a mob eager to keep the party going. A barricade at the bottom of North Eighth manned by cops turns us back and we head south down Wythe. A block away from the waterfront condos the housing stock speaks of a very different past, four-story rows sided in vinyl or tar paper. It could be a blue-collar enclave in any old industrial town except that the occupants of these railroad apartments are as likely to have graduated from Yale as the University of the Streets.

I'm trying to explain how things used to be on the Northside but it's not working. 'This used to be' is not the easiest game to play. That upscale seafood restaurant? It used to be a Jewish bakery with two-dollar loaves of heavy rye. The boutique window featuring a headless mannequin in funeral black? That was a friend's apartment, the windows painted over so that it was always midnight inside. By the time we make it back to the Edge, Beth is as tired of the game as I am. Broad walkways lead out to two new piers, metal clattering brightly to our footsteps. The disconnect from the old waterfront is overwhelming. A ferry service opened this summer on the East River and for the first time in over a century you can water-commute from Williamsburg to Midtown. Signs all down Kent Avenue announce the ferry arrival with one of the worst catchphrases I've ever read: 'Relax, we'll get you there,' straight verbal Valium. Four dollars takes you wherever the ferry goes—Long Island City, Wall Street, Governors Island. Stray concertgoers wander or sit on the patches of well-tended lawns. Dog walkers jabber into iPhones as their purebreds urinate on the well-tended lawns.

The Edge was built by the Stephen B. Jacobs Group, an architecture firm responsible for big Manhattan projects like the Hotels Giraffe and Gansevoort. In Manhattan, the Jacobs Group liked to supersize some classical form—Italianate, Federal, Georgian—and wrap it in a New Age glitter of mirrored glass and pulsing neon, mansard roofs mating with flying saucers. In Williamsburg, with no historical societies to placate, they could dispose of tributes to the olden days. Welcome to Abu Dhabi! (Or Key West, where Jacobs erected a white elephant of a hotel.) It was pointless to hate a large chunk of concrete and steel but I tried. Why? I mean, why build this thing? It didn't have anything to do with the place where it had been planted. You had the views, sure, but the East River isn't the the Gulf of Mexico—no sandy beaches and swimming only for iron men and suicides. When you walked out of the Edge you were still in the world of the Edge—street-level version—a dull chain of franchise stores and overpriced restaurants. The blessing of New York congestion was that when you left your house you were tossed into all those other people. People in the streets and in the stores and walking their dogs and running errands. Life. But when you walked out of the Edge you walked into nothing. Cars and trucks running down Kent and a few pedestrians but no city life and blocks to go before you found any. Outside even the plushest Upper West Side manor the city enveloped you. But at the Edge you had all the boredom of the suburbs without any of the trees. Only a methodical calculus could explain the choice to buy there—a certain kind of person with a certain income could afford to buy a certain number of square feet more at the Edge than he could on Water Street, and, after subtracting for the longer commute, you still had a reasonable investment opportunity. The views and the cool zip code were just throw-ins.

In the wake of another couple, we pass the last Edge tower on a walkway that wraps a former warehouse. Unlike the Edge, the warehouse wasn't designed by Jacobs, et al. The Austin, Nichols & Company Warehouse building is a stolid white cube that was built in 1915. Austin, Nichols has been disemboweled since I left the neighborhood, a 'gut reno,' and now offers loft rentals. Five thousand a month will get you eight hundred square feet.

This used to be all artists' lofts, I say. They had these amazing parties, over entire floors. There was a seawall here too with an iron gate. In the old days, boats could dock right at the building. We used to crawl underneath—it was just a huge open space—and then walk out to what was basically a forest.

I wave out at the remodeled piers.

When the Edge started construction, I say, they fenced all this off but we kept cutting holes in the fences. I guess they won.

I trail off at the glaze that films Beth's eyes, cataracts of boredom. My lost world is far from the ineluctable now, which at the moment provides us a view into a 'fitness center' on the ground floor of the former warehouse—a half acre of the most advanced pound-shredding, bun-rounding devices known to the twenty-first century in a space where railroad cars used to roll. Inside, fluorescent lights banish every shadow, but the room is empty, a display case.

'Where are you leading me?' slurs the man ahead of us. The couple is young and the man is handsome. His slur is half liquor, half Castile, a mellow blend. The girl giggles and I see they've hit another barrier, this one temporary, fresh plywood blocking the way to North Third. Over the plywood rises the round mass of a fuel storage tank. The couple turns back and we follow, all the way out of the Edge and out to Kent. Beth is ready to be somewhere else. She mentions the Greenpoint Tavern. I tell her it's still open. She asks if it's as tacky as it used to be. I assure her that it is, that you can still get a thirty-two-ounce Styrofoam cup of Bud for three dollars.

But there's one last place I want to show her. She humors me so we walk down Kent to North Third. I have it figured out: I'll point out the abandoned fuel tanks of New England Petroleum and then take her past Grand Ferry Park, where ferries stopped before the Williamsburg Bridge was built—a few more 'this used to be's' and then over and out. The tour will end with a whimper.

On North Third we face the usual obstacles. There's another fence, chain-link, and a string of lights dangling from a scaffold over the sidewalk. Underfoot, cobblestones, very different from the slick walkways on the Edge side of the plywood, Miami Beach to industrial ruin in a matter of inches. In an economic downturn that has people muttering 'Depression,' the Edge is only 40 percent sold, still a more robust figure than any of its rivals in the neighborhood can claim. Banners on Austin, Nichols offer rental lofts but most of the windows are dark. In recent years a security guard has barred the end of North Third but I don't see him tonight. This is our chance.

Come on, I say and hop over what my father told me was a 'Jersey barrier' when they first started appearing on the freeways in the seventies.

Where are you going? Beth says, but she follows. I expect shouts and men in uniforms, but we reach the end of the block without a sound. Just as I remember, the chain-link fence beside the fuel tanks is cut and sagging, and we duck through. A narrow walkway runs alongside the massive fuel tank and we reach another barrier, a solid metal panel, but ripped away from its top joint. We squeeze through and shuffle out along the walkway.

Still no shouts, no cops. After the second barrier I feel relief but we're still visible from the shore. The walkway is eighteen inches wide and algal pools of water make it slick. We turn a corner and continue our cautious shuffle, shoulders pressed against the cool white of the tank until we're past any shore sight lines. Safe at last. In front of us, wooden piers finger out to a series of docks.

Let's go up to the top, I say.

I lead Beth to a gate at the foot of a stairway that climbs the hundred-odd feet of the fuel tank. Wire—razor and barbed—crowns the high gate and fence. Beth is dubious.

I'll go first, I say, and clamber up the gate (if you have to climb a fence, take the gate—more footholds). Beth follows but freezes at the top. The cutoffs mean she has to swing her bare legs over the razor loops, one and then the other, fifteen feet over the ground.

I don't know if I can do this, she says.

Sure you can, I say. You already did the hard part.

That's easy for you to say, she says. You're not wearing Daisy Dukes.

She gears herself up and makes the move. No rusty slash, no tetanus scare. I've always loved exploring the waterfront but it's a hundred times better with a partner.

I'm not at all surprised that Beth hopped the fence; she did make it to the finals in the Golden Gloves. Eight years ago, Beth and I ate magic mushrooms before a night of dancing at Black Betty. On the way to the club, Beth thought it would be funny to hit me as hard as she could. We'd walk a few yards, then she'd spin around and drop a right in my stomach. I'd shout 'Are you crazy?' before hitting her back. After Black Betty, we ended up at my apartment. Her nice Jewish boyfriend—later husband, later ex-husband—watched in horror as we kept tagging each other on the couch. The next day the couple drove to see Beth's parents, and the boyfriend had to explain that he wasn't the person who'd painted her in bruises.

After the trek up the metal stairway we clamber through a maze of pipes and valves and hoses and walkways set in pebbled tar. I haven't been up here since I left Williamsburg and I notice changes. For one thing, lit bulbs drooping from extension cords like glass fruit make me think the late shift is about to clock in. There also seems to be more open space, as if they've been clearing the top of the tank. Here, too, demolition is under way.

The Williamsburg skyline has also changed, moving from the nineteenth to the twenty-first century in one five-year leap. From our perch we look across the entire three square miles or so of neighborhood: the old domed banks, the churches with their small-town spires, the flat black warehouse roofs, the LEGO squares of one-family houses, the steel bridge and cemetery beyond. To the north, the Edge is the most stunning irruption of the new, the three towers and piers and plazas an alien graft, Williamsburg-cum-cyborg. Other developments have sprung up along the waterfront, a patchwork of glass and burnished steel rising over brick factories and row houses clad in vinyl.

Traditionally, Williamsburg has been divided into three sections: Northside, Southside and East Williamsburg. When outsiders, all those German, Spanish, Japanese tourists, all those travelers from anywhere America, when they say 'Williamsburg,' they mean the Northside. The Northside is where the L subway stops first and where most of the restaurants, clubs and boutiques have sprouted. The Northside also has the best stretch of East River waterfront and landmarks like the Domino Sugar factory and the McCarren Park Pool. The Northside is where I lived for fourteen years and where the biggest changes have come.

My personal Northside runs from the river on the west to the great wall of the Brooklyn–Queens Expressway to the east. We can see the BQE from where we stand, a twisting line of headlights suspended in midair, glow-in-the-dark dragon several miles long. North, my neighborhood ends at McCarren Park, in the night a thirty-five-acre black moat below the lights of Greenpoint. The southern boundary of the Northside is said to be Grand Street, where the street prefixes change from north to south. My personal neighborhood goes further south than that, past an industrial zone of tenements and towering warehouses, all the way down to the elevated subway lines over Broadway and the Williamsburg Bridge. For fourteen years that was home but it never will be again.

From the bridge, we turn back toward the warehouse across North Third. The scenic view from the Austin, Nichols balconies takes in the fuel tanks, immense ghost of Williamsburg past. At eye level some thirty-five feet away is what looks like a dinner party—five people at a butcher-block table with bottles and candles. On top of the tank, Beth and I are exposed but since they don't expect us to be there, we're invisible. At my feet a slate block imperfectly covers a hole with a ladder leading down into the tank. A faint smell of petroleum and chemicals rises from the hole, the ladder a pathway to the underworld.

I want to take Beth to the fuel tank on the other side of the compound. We approach a catwalk that crosses the yard to the opposite tank. A few echoing steps onto the catwalk grate and I freeze: two security guards are talking below in the light of their checkpoint booth. Beth and I have been loud, practically shouting, and I'm sure we'll be spotted. I wonder if we can run back to North Third before a squad car arrives. As I have a couple of outstanding warrants, I'm not in any position to be arrested. The guards don't look up, though, and we creep out over the checkpoint. Across Kent a party has spilled out of another warehouse. The Monster Island Arts Center hasn't been absorbed by new Williamsburg yet, graffiti a splotched second skin over old brick. None of the partyers notice us and we're free to explore the other tank—more pipes and valves and giant faucet wheels that you'd need Hercules to turn.

Curiosity satisfied, we cross the catwalk again, tromp back down the stairs and climb the gate—no problem for Beth this time. I'm no longer disappointed with the night.

We run out on piers to the docks, massive cylinders plunging into the river muck. The docks hold storage sheds and rubber-wheeled carts and concrete mooring pegs as thick around as sumo wrestlers. I try to imagine the thick cables that wrapped the pegs and the big freighters rising behind them.

Beth points to one of the sheds.

You could live out here, she says. No one would know.

It's probably the only place in Williamsburg I can still afford, I say.

We sit on the dock edge, feet hanging over the water. Tour boats slide by, festooned with light. It's so quiet we can hear conversations on the boats, people at the railing taking it all in. A breeze stirs Beth's hair, the tips of her curls gilded by summer.

It's so quiet here, she says.

That's what I love about it, I say.

Across the river the skyline, bright Manhattan dream. Beth stares at the city and gently kicks the air.

It's crazy that you can be so close to all that and have it be so quiet, she says.

I don't feel melancholy at all. Breaking and entering doesn't give you time to cry over the past. Now my Williamsburg belongs to Beth too.

1

Dark City

1988–1994

The explosion cracked the summer evening. Light flash and then smoke rising. Another crack and flash, and another, four in all, shredding air and reverberating in the basin of the empty pool. The two camera people watched, transfixed as the sound claps faded and smoke billowed around them. From somewhere in the cloud, a voice emerged.

You guys shot all that? Great. Let's get out of here.

The artist stepped out of the cloud.

Pack up your cameras, he said. Come on! We've got to move!

In 1990, a young filmmaker named Esther Bell made her first trip to Williamsburg. She'd been hired for a shoot by an artist named Stephen Bennett. All Bennett told her was that he had an art installation in the neighborhood, that it was at a local pool and that they'd need to be careful there. He also paid cash, half in advance. This was more than enough for

Esther—for a twenty-year-old scraping by in New York City on odd (sometimes very odd) jobs, any chance to make money with her Super 8 was progress.

Esther had come to New York for the same reason we all did—to get away from somewhere else. For Esther those somewheres were Columbia and Charleston, South Carolina. Even though she'd spent most of her life in South Carolina, she never thought of herself as a Southerner. Her mother, Sharon, was an army brat who grew up at Mark Twain Village in Germany. Sharon was twenty-two and working as a window dresser in Heidelberg when she got pregnant on a romantic Paris trip that didn't include prophylactics (her eighteen-year-old boyfriend was another window dresser). In a pre–sexual revolution romantic saga, Sharon's high school sweetheart, Randy Bell, who'd also grown up on the base, found out that Sharon was pregnant. Randy returned to Germany from Harvard Law School and the three young people decided that Sharon should marry Randy and go to America. When Esther was born, Randy put his name on the birth certificate. Nineteen years would pass before she met her biological father, when he visited her in New York with his boyfriend.

Randy Bell's career took him to South Carolina, where he became legal counsel for the governor and then, at age forty, a justice on the state supreme court. He also suffered from Fabry disease, which killed him at forty-nine. His social standing and his illness, along with his brimstone Southern Baptist heritage, made the household a stifling place. When Esther was fourteen her parents divorced and Sharon moved to Charleston. Esther lived a divided life over the next few years—sharing a rowdy adolescence with her mother in a condemned house in Folly Beach, Charleston, while in Columbia, Anglophile, seersucker-wearing Randy wife tried to mold Esther into a belle.

Esther picked rebellion. Putting out a zine into the indie rock world, and she got to kno that passed through Charleston (and managed to keep her cool when Mike Ness from Social Distortion started sucking his own dick during an interview). Music led her to feminism and a style of her own. In her senior year of high school, Judge Bell agreed to pay her college tuition, but there were caveats—it had to be a religious institution, less than $2,000 a year, not in a city, and he would select all her classes. Being a lawyer, he drew up a contract and Esther spent her freshman year at Iona College, a small Catholic school in the Westchester town of New Rochelle. ('Idiots on North Avenue,' Esther says. 'They really were.') When Randy didn't hold up his side of the contract and pay the tuition, Esther was set free. She dropped out of Iona and enrolled in City College, smack in the middle of Harlem.

Williamsburg didn't look anything like New York to Esther, as Bennett led her and a second photographer—this one shooting video—down Bedford Avenue, past a shabby park to a brick castle surrounded by razor wire. Brush brambled the fences and graffiti covered every span of brick. Bennett had carved a way through the obstacles. 'What he'd done,' Esther says, 'was he'd taken a torch and made a hole in the fence.'

They crawled through and Bennett sealed the breach, then hurried them away from the eyes of the street. Inside the walls was a pool like no other Esther had ever seen before. Three regulation Olympic pools laid side by side would have sunk into the McCarren basin, which had a capacity for sixty-eight hundred dripping souls. Neglect had drained

pale blue interior. Debris and filth littered the cracked
concrete and a copse grew out of the diving pool.

Six years earlier the Northside fathers had solved their
integration woes by breaking the toy rather than sharing it.
In Williamsburg, Poles and the Irish, Jews and Italians, could
swim together, but when brown people wanted in, the water
was drained and the pool closed for good.

This was pre–cell phones, Esther says. And I started
thinking about how nobody in the world knew I was there
with this strange artist guy.

As she waited near the deep end, she didn't see anything
that looked like an art installation. You couldn't spook Esther easily—she was fit and brave and German solid, with a
defiant mane of bright red hair. Still, she wondered what
she would do if something went wrong.

Her anxieties didn't ease when two disheveled men ap-
proached her and the video guy (Bennett had disappeared).
They all started talking. The men told Esther that they were
Vietnam vets and on their way home from work. Home?
Home was under the pool, in a subterranean maze of corri-
dors and pipes. And they weren't the only people who found
the catacombs useful. 'Sure,' the vets told Esther. 'The Mafia
dumps bodies down there.' They claimed to have seen the
corpses.

As the sun set the vets moved on and Bennett was still
missing. Esther wondered if she would have enough light to
shoot the art, whatever it was. She didn't plan to stick around
after dark.

Just then Bennett came running toward them, shouting,
'Turn your cameras on! Turn your cameras on!'

Before he reached them, there was an explosion. And
then another one. Four powerful blasts from the top of the

keep that guarded the entrance, brilliant flashes and the smell of powder and gray smoke flowing over them.

Thankfully I had kept my finger on the trigger, Esther says, because it was a huge explosion and scared the shit out of us. The other guy didn't keep his finger on the trigger, so I was the only one who actually documented it. These weren't M-80s or firecrackers—the explosions were huge.

When the smoke cleared, Bennett pushed them toward the street. 'Let's go! Let's go! Let's go!' They ran to the fence and Bennett closed the gap behind them. As they walked away, angling for invisibility, Esther expected sirens, police cars, fire engines to confront the swimming-pool Armageddon. Instead, there was silence.

It was as if four explosions going off was normal, Esther says. Just another day in Williamsburg.

Bennett would use Esther's footage in a performance piece at ABC No Rio, a Lower East Side art space. On the train ride back to Manhattan, Esther worried about the effect of the explosions on the vets making dinner in the catacombs.

How decadent, Esther says. That was what I was thinking. How decadent. Here are these guys who need a real home and they're probably having flashbacks while this guy is making his art show.

Getting off the L at the Bedford stop put you on guard. From First Avenue the train took forever to pass under the tidal strait, too much time to worry about the tons of seawater and mud waiting overhead to crush you. The Bedford station was a bleak hole. The shit-brown paint was cracked and peeling. Rats scurried between the rails and dashed across the platform. Foul water dripped. Upstairs, Bedford Avenue wasn't any better. At seven p.m. you felt fear in the gloom and rightly so. Old New York hands donned their city armor. The street was quiet but not with the sprinkler hiss of summer lawns: no, Williamsburg was a ghost town. The other folks who got off the subway with you, most of them blue-collar men, hurried down the street, slipped around corners, disappeared. If you were curious, though, if you couldn't help yourself, you slowed down. You liked the jolt, the city edge; you wanted to see the ruins. Except for the flashing Christmas lights of the Greenpoint Tavern, Bedford Avenue was dark. Shutters masked the storefronts. Some had folding lattice gates instead of metal shutters so you could look inside. Behind the shutters, dust coagulated on display platforms. Merchants had locked their shop doors one day and never come back.

Three guys I knew moved to a Williamsburg loft in the summer of 1988: Stephan Schwinges, Kai Mitchell and Andrew Lichtenstein. They were perfect fodder for a rough neighborhood—young and cocky and willing to live on scraps. Drew and Kai had graduated that spring from Sarah Lawrence College just outside the city, and Stephan was a louche German expat who'd left his homeland under a cloud and bounced from Berlin to London and then to the East Village.

A Mexican American illustrator told Stephan that he was giving up the loft he shared with his wife in Williamsburg, a big space, two thousand–plus square feet for a thousand bucks a month, if Stephan was interested.

Stephan's response: 'Where the fuck is Williamsburg?'

But he went out and looked at the loft: two floors on the west side of a warehouse at the corner of Metropolitan and Driggs, right on the border between Northside and South.

The back windows looked out onto an even bigger warehouse and a weed-strangled lot. Catty-corner on Driggs was a stoneyard with winches and cables to hoist blocks of marble and granite. An Italian mason occupied the first floor of the warehouse on the other side of Metropolitan. Along the broad avenue warehouses overshadowed a few old tenements. No restaurants, no bodegas, no bars, no trees, nowhere to shelter from winter chill or summer blaze.

Stephan liked it just fine. 'It was good for me,' Stephan says, 'because I was a broke, broke artist type.' The loft gave him more for his money than the straitened dump he was paying fourteen hundred for on Ninth and B across from Tompkins Square Park. Anyway, things weren't working out too well with his girlfriend there. Stephan knew that Drew was looking for a place, and Drew brought in Kai.

None of them fit the neighborhood profile. As Drew says: 'If I walked out the back door I was in the Dominican Republic and if I walked out the front door I was in Poland.'

The Mexican American artist had a good reason to leave: his wife had been raped a few blocks away, near P.S. 17 on North Fifth and Berry. He wanted out, back home to the palm trees and sunshine of San Diego. Stephan wasn't put off by the horror story, though, or by the desolate streets. Nor were his future roommates. They were young and they were men: they felt inviolable.

Besides, in 1988 New York, few places outside of Gracie Mansion were safe. Danger was a price you paid to live there. A crack house near Stephan's apartment held open and thriving commerce. Stephan being Stephan, he walked into the crack house one drunken night and handed out bottles of Guinness to the dealers. After a 'What the fuck?' moment, the crack dealers drank Stephan's beer and they all became friends.

Things Fell Apart

'I want to get to Bellona and—'
—Samuel R. Delany, *Dhalgren*

Samuel Delany's 1975 novel *Dhalgren* is set in an American city disordered in time and space. An event horizon keeps phone calls and television broadcasts from entering or leaving 'Bellona,' which is covered in perpetual cloud. One night the clouds part to reveal two moons. The next day, a giant red sun rises, terrifying people until the cloud cover returns. Street signs and landmarks shift constantly and nobody remembers the last time he slept. Buildings burn for weeks without collapsing and gangs roam the nighttime streets, the gang members hidden within holographic projections of insects and monsters. Residents rely on stores of canned food and bartered goods to survive. Newcomers to dying Bellona are young drifters and loners; Delany's amnesiac protagonist is called Kid. One of his only memories is of having spent time in a mental hospital.

Delany puts Bellona in the Midwest but to me it feels like his hometown of New York City. It's not just anywhere in New York, though—not the mansions of West Side Drive or the glass mountains of Wall Street, not the fetid blocks around Times Square. Delany writes about the margins—empty streets, abandoned buildings, feral teenagers and ordinary civilians trying to negotiate the collapse. Images of Bellona rippled across the country, thrilling us in movie theaters and living rooms. It was the city of *Taxi Driver*, where Travis Bickle watched a liquor store owner shoot a robber and then helped him dump the body into the street. That was the city I came to, except a decade had passed, the fires had burned out, and the nation had elected a professional actor to the White House.

As a teenager, I lived with Reagan Junior—my brother watched *Rambo: First Blood* a thousand times and hung the Stars and Stripes, and a Catholic cross, over his bed. Reagan's world seemed upside down to me, but to my brother, I was the freak walking on the ceiling. In my world *Born in the U.S.A.* was about the suffering of a Vietnam vet; for my brother it was the anthem of America triumphant. In *Rambo* a Vietnam veteran's abuse at the hands of small-town cops causes him to have flashbacks to a Vietnamese prison camp; for my brother, John Rambo celebrated the red, white and blue. My brother was an Eagle Scout; I got kicked out of the same Boy Scout troop. We couldn't both be right, and who was I? A punk who landed in detention every day. Reagan never got into trouble (although my brother did); in fact, Reagan's polytetrafluoroethylene carapace earned him the nickname 'the Teflon president.'

All I had to fight Reagan were facts—in 'Born in the U.S.A.' Bruce Springsteen sings:

> *Out by the gas fires of the refinery*
> *I'm ten years burning down the road*

The story of a man haunted by prison and with 'nowhere to go' didn't sound like victory to me, but if everyone thinks you're wrong, does it really matter if you're right?

The kids in my high school AP classes pledged allegiance to *The Official Preppy Handbook*: to pin-striped oxfords, deck shoes, khakis and Ivy League idolatry. The handbook was a bestseller, the prep look adopted by kids who lived far from Newport yachts. The middle classes had imitated the rich for centuries but at some point they turned toward the masses—blue jeans and T-shirts, biker jackets and sneakers. *The Preppy Handbook* represented a paradigm shift but it made perfect sense in a country where, once again, greed was good.

Punk rock had a different take on fashion. Some of my friends donned safety pin earrings and purple Mohawks but to me, the clothes mattered less than the music. American A&R men had expected punk to be the next big thing. Boy were they wrong, but that was just fine with us. Postpunk politics included all kinds of tribes—old-school feminists and fuck-me feminists, vegetarians, anti-nuke folk and plenty of flat-out kooks. A Trotskyist friend of mine ran the music collective at Bard College and I trundled up there to hear the Minutemen one month and Doc Watson the next. Punk rock saved my life.

Reagan hated and feared and neglected the cities, so the city became the perfect place to get away from him.

Drew had been to Brooklyn exactly once before he moved there. This was not unusual for immigrants who'd come to New York for Manhattan. When the L crossed the river the color-coded subway map read like Sanskrit: Montrose, Morgan and Aberdeen stations were Atlantis, Ys and Shangri-La. Brooklyn was terra incognita with Mike Tyson replacing the sea monsters on the margins of ancient maps. Only a mistake would send you to East New York or Brownsville, where little kids wielded Glocks. Much better to shiver and watch the horror show on TV.

But if you were twenty-three and looking to get started in the big city without a trust-fund teat? If you were a daredevil who could walk into a crack house with a sack full of Guinness and figure it would turn out okay? Then maybe Brooklyn was the place for you. In 1988, $333.33 a month was no small nut for a freelance kid but Stephan, Drew and Kai didn't have any better offers. They took the loft.

Stephan appointed himself master builder and director of operations.

I had all these great ideas, he says. I told them, 'We're going to redo the walls. We're going to redo the floors.'

At first, renovation seems easy. You tool up. You read books, you look at diagrams, you talk to carpenter friends. Maybe one summer you apprenticed as a helper on a construction crew. So the circular saw whines, the sledgehammer cracks and walls of plaster and lath go down. Sheetrock spans the rubbled rooms.

Then reality hits: you have to live in a ruin. Gypsum dust spreads everywhere, boot prints tracking across the floors. The dust follows you to bed and turns your hair into steel wool. One day you're poking at wires in an electrical panel when sparks shoot up your arm and the building goes dark for twelve hours. You fumble plumb bob and chalk line and finally put up framing of stud and track but there are gaps, gaps you try to mud with heavy applications of joint compound ('We kind of fucked up the walls,' Stephan says). Crude portals gape between rooms.

To pay for the renovations you have to make money, so the work drags on for months. Pipes jam from the odd clots that find their way into the sink. Lukewarm water trickles out of a spout in a shower grimed with plaster and paint. After two minutes lukewarm becomes ice cold. Paint smears you, turns gray and ruins clothes, and the nearest Laundromat is ten blocks away. Renovation costs much more than you thought it would. There is yelling. There is a nascent class struggle: 'Who made you the fucking boss of the world?' the workers grumble. Stephan is unapologetic: 'I took the biggest room. It was kind of the VIP lounge with the corner view. I found the place, so . . .'

Stephan wanted a spiral staircase up to his suite. Out came the circ saw. The hole carved through the ceiling dropped dead rats onto the kitchen floor. In photos, the boys look at you from behind goggles and masks, wary of asbestos and gypsum dust, of silicosis and cancer (Kai fends off the ceiling with an umbrella). The thin cotton masks were a poor defense, but twenty-four is about risk, especially for the testosterone-addled, the future a million miles away.

Trouble from Kreuzberg to Avenue B had prepared Stephan for life in Williamsburg. He'd left Düsseldorf for high school in Berlin and joined a radical student group. They protested against nuclear power. They protested against McDonald's 'restaurants' in Germany. 'We got into a lot of shit,' Stephan says. He caught beatings—beatings at demonstrations, beatings from skinheads, beatings from cops, beatings from model citizens who didn't appreciate his grubby band of radicals. When he found himself under police surveillance he decided it was time for a Wanderjahr.

London's East End brought more of the same: 'You would get robbed by Jamaicans and beat up by skinheads. I was kind of used to it by then.' A chance meeting with an American actor in a pub sent him to New York City. The actor had gone to college with Drew and they all met up on the Lower East Side. 'Drew's a cool guy,' the actor said. 'A photographer and an activist and troublemaker like you. You'll get along.' The actor was right.

Their landlord came from the old Italian neighborhood

that centered around the St. Vincent de Paul Roman Catholic Church on North Seventh and Driggs. Jean Paul, Sr., imported De Cecco pasta from his hometown in Italy.

In order to get into his office downstairs, Stephan says, you had to go through a dubious hallway, then climb through a giant hole. It was like something you'd see in war footage from Stalingrad. John Paul, Sr., would sit there at this old-fashioned shellacked wooden desk that probably weighed half a ton. He had all these cheesy sculptures of spaghetti, of forks holding spaghetti, all over the place, all these dubious awards for his spaghetti sauce and his olive oil. His sons were total characters. The younger one dressed like a thug, and the older one, Jean Paul, Jr., was always wearing some fancy Italian suit. I'd ask him, 'Why are you wearing this suit when you're working at the warehouse?' He'd tell me, 'I need to look good, alla the time.'

Despite the banging and crashing from the loft the landlord-tenant relationship ran smooth. The boys showed up at the office on the first of the month and paid their thousand dollars in cash (no lease, of course). Everybody was happy. Then Stephan got a new girlfriend. Suddenly the landlord was greatly interested in his tenants, and by the way, who was this black girl coming in and out of his building? They worked it out Old World–style, Stephan going downstairs with his girlfriend and introducing her to the John Pauls. Handshakes followed, and kisses on the cheek; harmony was restored.

As racist as the local Italians could be, their suspicion had helped to protect the Northside from the drugs that had devastated the Southside for decades. From his window, Drew looked down at the prostitutes who patrolled the Driggs-Metropolitan corner in miniskirts and stilettos no matter the weather. At night they huddled over crack pipes in his doorway and got annoyed when he tried to slide through. A Dominican pot dealer who grew up on the Southside told me the corner was so exposed and dangerous that he would go blocks out of his way to avoid it. But angel wings of ignorance protected the boys. Most of the time, anyway.

The only take-out Chinese for miles was on the Southside: South Second and Bedford—fried chicken and blackened eggrolls at ghetto prices. One night in 1990, Stephan called in his order, walked to the spot and was surrounded by three lowlifes as he left. Stephan didn't know about the heroin turf wars that roiled the Southside, but he knew he was in trouble.

They were totally fucked up on PCP or who knows what, he says. I only had five bucks left so I would defend my Chinese food. I said, 'Fuck you, you ain't getting my Chinese food.' So these guys pulled knives and chased me down the block. I ran back to the house and Drew said, 'Should we call the cops?' 'Call the cops!' I said. 'What are the cops gonna do?' I was a little bit shell-shocked. But we had a beer and everything was fine.

The loft was home but Williamsburg wasn't—it didn't offer enough. Drew fell in love with the Ship's Mast, a bar on the corner of North Fifth and Berry where artists and locals shared lasagna off a hot plate in the back. There was the Chinese place and a Dominican restaurant where Drew would get rice and beans. It also served as a fence. ('Every time I went there,' Drew says, 'guys would come in trying to sell car stereos or bicycles or random appliances. Three bucks for a brand-new Sunbeam toaster.') On Bedford between North Sixth and Seventh a Polish diner became notorious among the boys for the parsimony of its cream cheese schmear.

There'd been Poles in Greenpoint for a century, but perestroika brought a new influx and they pushed down into the Northside tenements and storefronts one step ahead of Stephan and the boys. The Italians preferred this group of fellow Catholics to the Puerto Ricans and let them buy in. On their morning trips to the bagel shop the boys ran up against the Eastern European adaptation to perpetual scarcity.

The girls there were coming straight from the airport, Stephan says, and they'd give us the thinnest layer of cream cheese. And we were like this: 'Ladies, first of all, this is America. We have mountains of motherfucking cream cheese. Do me a favor, because I am from West Germany, not EAST Germany like your Communist comrades. Can you put some freaking cream cheese on that?'

That was Williamsburg for the émigré artist. To get to an ATM, a café or a bookstore you took the L to First Avenue and headed south. The Lower East Side was the place to hit a club, to grab a falafel, to stare at pretty girls who might appreciate your mix tapes (like all frontiers, the Northside suffered from a dearth of beddable women). Manhattan was also the place you got paid: Stephan did commercial photography and worked as a studio manager and assistant for some big-name photographers. Drew's photojournalism skills scored him freelance gigs for *The Village Voice* and *The City Sun*, a Brooklyn-based African American paper that covered the real life of the city. Most days they shuttled out of the loft early in the morning and only came back after drinks somewhere downtown. Kai, alas, was generally depressed. He painted his room psych-ward green and rarely left it.

Both the *Voice* and the *Sun* had Monday deadlines so Drew would spend Sunday processing film in the bathroom, which he converted into a darkroom. 'I just put a wooden board over the bathtub and laid the chemicals out on that,'

Drew says. The darkroom was compensation. 'Drew's bed-room was the size of a place where you put a broom,' Stephan says. 'I was surprised he was able to lay down. It had the shittiest back window with an awful view of a big gray wall. But hey, he was happy. He was a simple man.' Drew worked late into Sunday night and then ran out on Monday morning to deliver his photos.

Drew covered the aftermath of the Yusuf Hawkins murder for the *Voice* and photographed a Bensonhurst demonstration where the white locals proudly presented watermelons to his camera. He covered the Sharpton marches for the *Sun* and got a photo of the reverend being stabbed in the chest. Later he shot the reaction to Gavin Cato's death and the Crown Heights riots that followed.

There was a lot of anger and a lot of raw energy in city neighborhoods then, Drew says. But at the same time, New Yorkers didn't always act like you might expect. They were almost more . . . thoughtful than people in the rest of the country. I remember being on the subway after the Rodney King verdict came down in Los Angeles, watching us all watch each other with an uneasy awareness. The merchants pulled down their shop grates in the morning in anticipation, and yet the peace held.

Williamsburg didn't share the anger or the energy and stayed quiet. For Drew it was a place to recover before he rushed out again.

Walk quickly from the subway to the loft. Don't look at anyone. Don't come alone.

Kai and Drew and Stephan were having a housewarming party, and the caveat came with the invitation.

Before the party, Kai told me he'd gotten jumped one

night as he got off the L. He threw the attacker to the ground and ran. He didn't report it to the cops. They would have said: 'What do you expect us to do? This is New York. Do you know how many times this happens every day? Just feel lucky that you got away.' Kai's story didn't surprise me: every time I went to the city it seemed like someone tried to rob or hustle me.

My new girlfriend and I got a ride to the party with an acquaintance from college. At eighteen I'd arrived at Sarah Lawrence, a thirty-minute train ride away from Grand Central Station. College was better than Catholic high school but I often felt as different from the art-school kids as I had from guidos and suburban jocks. My art-school peers had gone to performing arts schools and private academies. Their parents were professors, or painters, or gazillionaires. They summered in Europe while I mowed lawns in Rhode Island. Where I lacked train fare, they went to the Russian Tea Room, gambled in illegal casinos and scored heroin in Alphabet City. Most of the time, I had to settle for secondhand stories: 'It was a ballroom in the thirties . . . The bartender has a black eye patch . . . The room is full of antiques and has mahogany wainscoting . . . There was this transvestite wearing a tartan kilt and carrying a lunchbox with peanut-butter-and-honey sandwiches . . .' The city became a backdrop in my dreams—looming towers, orange shimmer on the horizon, the oily black river—but it was out of reach. I wanted to get all the way in; I wanted my own room in the maze.

I dropped out of college after my sophomore year because I was screwing up—partying too much, skipping classes, even getting banned from school concerts for bad behavior. A year of failure in Southern California, including being fired from six jobs, sent me back to school. It was different the second time around: I wrote the papers, I spoke up in class and the professors noticed. For the first time in my life, adults approved of me. All the lights had turned on and everything made sense—*The Interpretation of Dreams*, *Madame Bovary*, accounts of the Chumash genocide in Santa Barbara. Book smarts gave me something; next to Shakespeare and Hegel, freebasing in Daddy's brownstone was less alluring. It didn't seem so important that I'd never been to Paris or that my dad wasn't a Hollywood mogul.

Confidence brought me a different city. A friend had a seven-hundred-dollar apartment on the corner of Thirteenth and B at the end of a block of squats. I'd crash on his couch and we'd shoot pool in Puerto Rican bars and hang out in Tompkins Square Park. He showed me a city you didn't have to be rich to live in.

I don't remember much about Drew's housewarming party, probably because Sarah and I were drinking in the car. I do remember the ride down the Major Deegan into the gravity well of the city, across the titanic bridges and roadways, the buildings packed together, the orange sky without a single star. But instead of taking the Third Avenue Bridge and dropping into the video game of the FDR Drive we turned east and passed over low rows of houses. Some of the tiny backyards had aboveground pools like ships in a bottle.

Are you sure this is the right address? Aliya said. She was a gorgeous Egyptian whose family owned half the Nile or the pyramids or a couple of deserts. Her English had the clear tone of Swiss boarding schools.

Silence met us when we opened the car doors on Metropolitan. This wasn't a city I knew. Big buildings loomed, the windows dark. Every other streetlamp was out. I saw someone leaning against a wall, a woman, cigarette ember in her shadow face.

I'm worried about my car, Aliya said. That made sense: there weren't any other cars on the street.

We rang the buzzer. Nothing. We rang again. Upstairs a cube of light beckoned. The woman detached herself from the wall and sauntered up to a streetlamp. She had dark skin, golden bangles and a very short dress. Aliya reached into her purse and dragged out an object that I only realized was a phone when she started talking into it. (It was 1989 and I'd never seen a cell phone before.)

Yes, she said. We're right outside.

The door opened and there was Kai, smiling. We went inside as fast as we could, up a broken staircase into warmth and music.

On the ride home, Sarah took my hand and said, 'I think we're going to make it.' She was right, but only for a while. We got a sublet that summer in Brooklyn Heights and I found a job working for an aspiring slumlord in Red Hook, a neighborhood so desolate it made Williamsburg seem like *Mister Rogers' Neighborhood*. I started to feel at home in the other city. But my first visit to Williamsburg was the last I'd make for years.

Chris Miskiewicz

After his shift at Trunz Meat Market on Metropolitan Avenue, Chris walked to the waterfront. It was pouring rain, all the streetlamps were broken and he was miserable. At the deli, an older coworker had bullied him in the basement, the way he did on every shift. Rob tripped Chris, knocked supplies out of his arms and sucker punched him in the kidneys. Once Rob shoved Chris into the trash compactor and turned it on. It was the resentment a man going nowhere felt for a kid who still had a chance.

Chris stepped out on the India Street pier toward the Manhattan lights, his trench coat and combat boots providing some insulation from the weather. His hair—long in the front, short in the back—flopped into his eyes. There weren't many kids in the neighborhood who dressed like Chris. Guido ruled the Northside—Guido with his open white shirts and gold chains, Guido with his cuginettes and Camaros. Neighborhood girls forged skyscraper bangs in clouds of Aqua Net and Chris eyed them with hopeless lust.

Half Italian, half Polish, Chris couldn't have been more of a local. His mother had been born in Williamsburg, as had her mother, on North Eighth Street. At thirteen his grandmother had started working a foot press, a job she kept even as turning out clips for handbags became turning out clips for guns in World War II—same machine, same clip. Chris's Italian grandfather found a post as a runner on Wall Street during the Depression, for the dazzling wage of forty-four dollars a week, until spinal meningitis felled him on the trading floor. He woke up deaf in the hospital and went back to work at the Silvercup Bakery, an enormous bread factory in Long Island City.

After Chris's parents divorced, his mother raised him in various apartments across the Northside and Greenpoint—Sutton Street, Richardson, Henry, North Tenth for a while. Moving was easy in New York those days—people swapped apartments like baseball cards.

Despite his Northside bona fides, Chris never fit in, not from his days at St. Cecilia's on a block-long Catholic compound hard by the BQE (Polish kids went to St. Stanislaus, but the divorce put Chris in the Italian camp) to Monsignor

McClancy Memorial High School in Jackson Heights. Chris's social handicaps? He read books and lacked a Brooklyn accent. Chris credited his grandfather's deafness for his diction: 'I remember this conversation,' Chris says, 'where my mom was like, 'Ya gotta look in Grandpa's eyes and enunciate everything when ya talk ta him so he can understand cuz he's a lip reader and he can't hear your fuckin' words.' I was like, 'All right. I got it.' A few months before his pier walk, an acquaintance had taken exception to Chris's version of English:

I remember Pete Seppi coming up to me and saying, 'Why you talk so weird?' 'I don't know,' I said. 'What do you mean?' 'Ya accent, where are ya from, California?' 'No. And I actually speak correctly where you sound like a fool.'

Like a lot of disagreements in Williamsburg, this one ended with violence. 'So he just starting throwing punches at my face,' Chris says.

On the pier end, Chris squatted and lit a joint. He knew the pier well—one of his mother's boyfriends, a fuckup named Kevin McCarthy, had bragged to an eight-year-old Chris about stealing cars. According to Lynch, they would get a car on Friday night and drive it around all weekend. Then on Sunday they'd brick the gas pedal and launch the car off the pier. 'There were a lot of guys in the neighborhood like that,' Chris says. 'Guys who'd been to Vietnam and basically lived in the local bars and the OTB.'

Chris huddled over the joint. As the resonating warmth of marijuana lifted him, the rain slackened. He looked across the river. Manhattan there, indecipherable script in the lit windows of the Midtown towers and in the sentry blocks of public housing, all under an orange sky raggedly domed by storm clouds. With the flashing insight of the stoned, Chris realized that every one of the lights in all those buildings meant people—one or five or ten people to a light, an entire embodied universe and he would never be a part of it. They were over there and he was stuck in a dead, empty town that seemed to have nothing at all to do with New York City.

I was just floored by the numbers, Chris says. All those people. And I was hit with this feeling that I'm late all the time.

Chris had good reason to believe that he'd been left behind—that was all the neighborhood talked about.

'Greenpoint sucks. Yeah, fucking Williamsburg sucks. It sucks heah.' You'd hear this from your parents. You'd hear it from your friends. You'd just heard it through family: 'It fucking sucks heah. Fuckin' oil.' Everyone hated living here. We all knew we were going to die of cancer. 'This fucking sucks. It sucks, it sucks, it sucks.' That's all you'd hear. You know: the bars suck, your neighbor sucks, everything's dirty, everything is full of garbage, the waterfront's destroyed. And it stunk. The shit factory STUNK.

The 'shit factory' was the Newton Creek Wastewater Treatment Plant. The plant, the largest of fourteen in New York City, has the capacity to treat over 300 million gallons of wastewater a day. The glass domes of the treatment plant loom over Greenpoint, science fiction mosques casting a soft blue light. On warm days when the wind blows south the smell of decomposing shit wafts over Greenpoint and the Northside.

It stunk, man! Chris says. You would go through the historic area like Milton Street, all that around St. Anthony's, and it smelled like every toilet was on fire.

His grandmother always talked about the day in 1950

when a reinforced concrete sewer exploded in the heart of Greenpoint, blowing manhole covers three stories high, shattering shop windows and blasting open ten feet of pavement at the intersection of Manhattan Avenue and Huron Street. It would be another twenty-eight years before anyone realized that the explosion had been caused by a massive oil spill. 'Massive' only begins to describe the thirty million gallons of the Newton Creek Spill. A toxic stratum of oil and sewage that one expert described as 'black mayonnaise' oozes under the entire neighborhood. The product of 140 years of industrial effluvia, the spill continues to vent benzene and methane gas into basements, streets and backyards.

We were in this dying industrial town, Chris says. Right across from the fucking UN. And nobody even realized we there.

Stephan was the first one to leave the loft. Girlfriends tire of sharing three-man bathrooms and a few weeks after Stephan got married he moved out. He stayed in Williamsburg, though, settling with his wife, Cherryl, in a run-down brownstone on South Sixth and Berry in the shadow of the Williamsburg Bridge.

The surrounding blocks highlighted Williamsburg's lost glory and its dismal present. On Broadway former banks with marble pillars and great domes rotted away like the temples of Angkor Wat. Yet limousines pulled up in front of the Peter Luger Steak House as if nothing had changed since the Roaring Twenties. Rising beside the bridge, the Domino Sugar plant operated under its forty-foot sign with a skeleton crew at a fraction of capacity. Decaying brownstones like Stephan's were shoehorned between enormous warehouses and rows of tenements. The bridge itself was falling apart, and decades of deferred maintenance had led to a temporary closure in 1988. Stephan and Cherryl were hardy, though, and on warm days they would bike to work over the bridge. Big gaps in the metal plates on the bike path showed the black slick river hundreds of feet below.

One night not long after they moved into the brownstone, Stephan came home to find two men in their apartment. One of the men ran and Stephan wrestled with the other before he escaped. On the way out, the men shouted that they'd be back. They said they were going to fuck Stephan up. They said they were going to kill him. However, Stephan's marriage had given him more than a wife. It had given him protection.

My father-in-law is a decorated New York cop, Stephan says. He has a moustache and wears a long leather coat. Just like Shaft. And he's a little bit crazy. My brother-in-law is also crazy.

A phone call brought the in-laws to Williamsburg. They arrived heavily armed.

I had my .38, Stephan says. My father-in-law had his two service revolvers. My brother-in-law had a Glock.

Stephan's foes were not hard to find.

So we rolled up, right to these guys at their hangout around the corner from Peter Luger. And I basically told them, 'Fuck with me, please. You'll see what happens.'

The show of force had positive results.

After that those guys were really sweet to me. One guy came by and gave me a present. He told me that his cousin was an idiot and promised he would never be any trouble. I was like, 'Cool. If you're cool, I'm cool. Let's smoke some green. Let's shut the fuck up.' After that I never had any problems in the neighborhood.

．

In June of the year Francis Fukuyama declared the end of history, *New York* magazine ran a feature: 'The New Bohemia over the Bridge to Williamsburg.' It wasn't the first piece that mentioned artists in Williamsburg, but it was the first one *about* artists in Williamsburg. The piece talked about Teddy's, the hundred-year-old bar on North Eighth and Berry, it mentioned 'a cross-dressing artist named Medea de Vyse' and all the crazy parties the crazy artists had—parties with infrared sensors and 'plastic fog,' parties in abandoned meat lockers with scrap metal streamers hung from ceilings. It offered lavish descriptions of swashbuckling bohemian fashion. A couple wearing '*Road Warrior* jackboots and earrings in every pierceable orifice' are carrying a bicycle wheel, 'no doubt . . . so they can weld it into a sculpture' (cuz those crazy artists wouldn't ride bikes). De Vyse posed in a red sheath dress at Teddy's, working-class regulars behind her indifferent as they nursed boilermakers. In a photo of the wrecked waterfront, a shirtless young artist smears paint on a giant canvas, Manhattan skyline in the distance. 'In the 70s, it was SoHo,' de Vyse said. 'In the 80s, the East Village. In the 90s, it will be Williamsburg.'

Through the haze of two decades, the article seems ancient, like something out of *Mad Men*. We're told that the waterfront determines artists' style, 'a sort of *Blade Runner* Industrial Gothic.' 'I heard they rent back rooms in working factory buildings, and that their beds are just a few feet away from these big booming machines,' a woman informs the writer at a 'SoHo cocktail party.' It all reminds me of my dad's World War II stories about the cardboard he put in his shoes to cover the punctured soles. What dates the *New York* article most of all is the fact that it's so goddamn long.

Five thousand words, maybe more, and it's not even a cover story!

Daniel Wurtzel, a sculptor friend of Drew's, moved to Williamsburg in 1989 for the obvious reason: cheap rent on a big space. As his tool kit included a quarter-tipped chain saw, he needed more space than most. In fact, he did his carving outdoors in a lot at Hope and Havemeyer. Although he tried not to pull the starter before eight a.m., he didn't worry about noise complaints—the artists' studios in the warehouse next door were all illegal.

After the *New York* article ran, people began to stop at the fence as he carved. When he dropped the dead man's switch and lifted his goggles, they'd wave him over. The visitors looked like they had fallen asleep on the L and gone one station too far.

Sorry to bother you, they'd say. I was just wondering if maybe you knew about spaces for rent around here.

Not really, Daniel would say, then slide down his safety goggles and get back to work.

Sarah and I went to San Francisco after her senior year. That was as far as we made it. Off a college campus, a boyfriend who writes incisive papers on Proust impresses exactly no one; Sarah left me so she could explore the options that come with being young, beautiful, charming and rich. Yet the boost from my professors propelled me through my twenties. College didn't teach me how to earn a living, but it did give me confidence; I was going to be a writer, no matter what.

A German friend offered me a free apartment in Munich. Next I moved to Paris because a woman I'd dated was in school there. Then my Trotskyist friend made me a long-distance sweat-equity offer: if I helped him renovate a loft on East Fourteenth Street, I could stay there rent-free. So I bounced back to New York City in 1993, the summer I turned twenty-seven. The loft got built out and I moved to 169th and Broadway.

The condo building where I rented a room was a relic of New York past, with a doorman and old Jewish tenants so frail that light filtered through them. Their tower was sinking into a Dominican sea—no one wanted to buy there, not in the crack days when so many Jersey boys came to score that cars backed up the George Washington Bridge ramps and every eleven-year-old on a mountain bike had a pager clipped to his belt. The uptown commute wore me out. After nights partying downtown, I'd fall asleep on the A and wake up on 207th Street, wondering what had gone wrong.

Williamsburg was the obvious next step, its equation mingling low rent, proximity to the Lower East Side and the first intimations of a new cool. If you were a free-floating twentysomething skidding along ley lines, you wanted to live on Avenue B but would settle for Bedford Avenue. Williamsburg was a dog whistle that people like me were starting to hear, summoning us from every corner of the city. The *New York* article was only the declaration of a self-evident truth: we couldn't afford the Village anymore.

This time my guide to Williamsburg was a cross-dressing filmmaker I'd met in San Francisco. During the week Ying wore business casual to his job managing containers on Chinese freighters. On weekends Ying favored spangled bustiers, dresses with spaghetti straps and expensive lipstick. (I remember one of his girlfriends borrowing a tube—was it 'Harlot Red'?—and saying, 'He buys better stuff than I do!') He wore a speculum on a cord around his neck; later, he replaced the speculum with a bicycle horn. One night I had to defend Ying from a bunch of Mexican guys who jumped out of a car on Broadway because he was so damn cute in his tight black dress. Ying introduced me to off-menu Chinese delicacies like crab roe and pig intestines and to wuxia films—we watched the young Jet Li fly across China-town screens. Ying's father was an officer in the Chinese navy and Ying had been in the Chinese merchant marine. When Ying's company transferred him from San Francisco to New York he ended up at the Tung Fa noodle factory in Williamsburg, where he had a makeshift studio.

Taking up most of Berry between South Fourth and Fifth, the noodle factory was a fourteen-story white mono-lith that had once teemed with sweatshops—a central feature in the city since the Civil War. A few of the sweatshops still operated and in the long hallways you'd see clothes racks and fabric scraps on the floors. At ten o'clock at night, weary Latin women would pass you on their way home. Open doors revealed dozens of similar women waist-deep in fabric, lean-ing over sewing machines.

Ying's first job in the U.S. was delivering pizza via bicycle but he quickly graduated to a big American car. He loved the plush upholstery and the fingertip steering of his Chrys-ler Fifth Avenue with a backseat the size of a twin bed (for a man of Ying's proclivities, the backseat came in handy). Like Drew and Stephan, Ying spent most of his time in Manhat-tan, and when he drove home to Williamsburg, he parked his car on Berry Street and hurried inside. The noodle factory was a retreat, cut off from the street, a place to hover near the city. Ying's studio had a large bed, a folding movie screen, tens of thousands of dollars' worth of film equipment—including a camera with a shutter speed so fast it had been designed to shoot rocket launches—and not much else. No matter how much Ying drank or how far we were from my apartment on 169th Street, he'd always drive me home.

Most nights out we made a last stop at Ying's loft with whatever party flotsam we'd picked up along the way. Film canisters, strips of film and empty cognac bottles littered his floor. Through the eleventh-story windows, J-M-Z subway cars clanked across the Williamsburg Bridge. The bridge lights and headlights made it look like Six Flags. A darker skyscape rose to the south, warehouses crowded together and behind the warehouses the grim towers of housing projects.

Watching the bridge and the Manhattan lights from Ying's studio, I didn't think about the streets. They were just an obstacle as we moved from car to building, our uneasiness vanishing when we sat cradled inside. It took a long time for me to realize that you couldn't have the freedom without the fear.

In the summer of 1994 I wrote a play for a downtown theater company, and when the director told me her friend Rose needed a housemate in Williamsburg, I jumped. Williamsburg *qua* Williamsburg still meant nothing to me, but I'd be closer to the action; no more passing out on the train.

Rose and I lived in a four-story tenement at the intersection of Union and Grand Streets, blocks east of the elevated corridor of the Brooklyn–Queens Expressway. The neighborhood was Dominican and Puerto Rican and our apartment perched over a Chinese-Spanish restaurant with the unlikely name of Apolo. Cockroaches waved from the walls and you mistook carapaces for Sichuan peppercorns, antennae for bean sprouts. Greasy air from the restaurant vent poured into my apartment, coating the walls. The corner location exposed us to the uproar on the street and the sledgehammer of summer. I used bedsheets for curtains and plugged my ears to get to sleep.

The other three corners sported a twenty-four-hour Mexican bakery, a twenty-four-hour Caribbean fried chicken joint, and a bodega that sold both heroin and crack. Those attractions brought customers through the night: black town cars with tinted windows double-parked, speakers booming, horns blaring, people shouting. The crackheads who smoked in my doorway at night would give me a gruff hello.

Rose had a schizophrenic mother and an unruly heroin habit. The two did not seem unrelated. She had gone to Reed College where she majored in art history and substance abuse. The graphic novels she wrote were beautifully drawn, meticulously plotted and never finished. Sketchbooks that ended in half-drawn panels piled up beside her bed.

All my New York apartments fit the same dismal profile: shabby rooms in rough neighborhoods. The neighborhoods weren't where I 'lived'; life went on in other places, all of them a subway ride away. On the weekends I'd take long walks and buy supplies—alien vegetables tumbled in outdoor bins and ghetto-mart carrion that looked scavenged from Dumpsters. I was a mote drifting on the surface of ethnic New York. That was the city you had to deal with if you were poor. You were ignored or you were in trouble, the latter more likely if you were white and lived in a black neighborhood. In Dominican Washington Heights, I was invisible, but in Fort Greene I was conspicuous. Sometimes it was funny, like when a sharp-dressed, red-eyed jazz musician spent fifteen minutes trying to figure out what a white boy was doing at the take-out Chinese on Lafayette at midnight. But there were also the guys who offered me Knicks tickets on Myrtle Avenue and then tried to drag me into an alley; when I walked by later they said, 'Maaaan, we were just joking!' There was the stoned teenager at the Lafayette Avenue station who, after muttering 'Fucking white people' and 'Yusuf Hawkins,' started throwing punches. I wanted to say, 'Hey, I'm on your side. What happened to Yusuf Hawkins was a terrible crime.' Instead I punched back.

Cabbies wouldn't cross the Williamsburg Bridge even though the law said they had to take you anywhere in the five boroughs. They hesitated because they couldn't get return fares, and because they were afraid. When I moved to Williamsburg, my older New York friends said: 'How can you live there? It's so dangerous.' They lived in rent-stabilized apartments in the Village or posh buildings on the Upper West Side. Brooklyn, except for gringo outposts in Park Slope and Brooklyn Heights, was to them a dark place—dark alleys, dark stories, dark people. Sometimes Manhattanites peered through the mesh of the Cyclone fence and wondered what happened on the other side.

A first cousin of mine, a stockbroker, came to New York around the same time that I did and bought a condo in a converted schoolhouse near Carroll Gardens. He hated and feared Brooklyn. The beauties of the borough were completely lost on Paul but I was beginning to see them.

The late-night subways and menacing streets thickened my skin. I got down that city walk—fast and direct—I got my subway lean; I got the hard city stare—but I also learned when to look away. I felt less like a potential victim. Fifteen minutes away from my Grand Street apartment on the other side of the BQE, I found a place filled with people who had come to Brooklyn on quests like mine.

2

A Bar in Hell

1995–1997

The most striking objects on the whole of Brooklyn's waterfront have yet to be mentioned. Just to the north of the Wallabout canal we come to the first of the series of sugar refineries, whose towering outlines on a foggy day, or in the last of the twilight, will suggest the lineaments of a Rhenish castle. We are here in the midst of the greatest sugar refining center in the world, where one establishment will sometimes in a single day convert 4,000,000 pounds of raw material into 12,000 barrels of refined sugar.

—*Brooklyn Daily Eagle*, July 30, 1883

January 1996

The first time I went to Kokie's Place they wouldn't let me in. From the outside, it was a drab brick tavern at the corner of North Third and Berry. When I pulled open the heavy door, a short Latino with Marcel waves carded me. I didn't have ID. You never needed one in Brooklyn.

But I'm thirty years old, I said.

The bouncer shrugged.

On the way home I muttered and scuffed my feet. I couldn't believe it—I'd gotten bounced from a coke bar named Kokie's.

The next time I made sure to bring the driver's license.

We're closing in fifteen minutes, the same sullen bouncer said. He was lying. The door opened and I stepped inside.

If you lived in Williamsburg you heard about Kokie's. 'It's a coke bar that opens on Thursday night and doesn't close again until Sunday afternoon.' Also, 'There are Puerto Rican gangsters and locals in there. They have these booths in the back with curtains covering them. People wait in line for the booths to do their coke.' I wanted to see it. New York City in 1996 had plenty of after-hours clubs that sold coke—it had plenty of grocery stores that sold coke—but I liked the hubris of 'Kokie's Place' on the awning.

That night I sat with a three-dollar ten-ounce Bud bottle and studied customers in the bar mirror: cackling middle-aged Latinas with high heels and big asses, a group of young Poles with buzz cuts, two guys in dusty overalls who looked like they had just gotten off a factory shift, and a couple of artist types with their sideburns and thick-framed glasses. It was an ugly room—gray concrete floors, a few pieces of neon, the windows grilled and shuttered. Fluorescent light splashing off the concrete made the bar even uglier. The back room had a few garage-sale tables and chairs. Curtains screened the famous booths but nobody lined up to use them. A hulking janitor with splayed teeth pushed a mop slowly across the floor.

In the previous two months, I'd lost my live-in girlfriend and then my job. Without income or Rebecca's half of the rent, I flirted with eviction. Urban survival skills kicked in—I jumped subway turnstiles and lived on Campbell's soup mixed with pasta. At the corner bodega, minestrone and tomato soups cost ninety-nine cents. Vegetable beef was my favorite but it cost a dollar nineteen. I ate minestrone. (No Top Ramen for me; I had standards.) Thirty years old and hoarding pennies. I wrote a piece about the joy of suicide for my column in *Cups: The Café Culture Magazine*. My subway reading was the Bible—1 Kings. The lavish descriptions of wealth in Kings appealed to me, as did God's fury: 'Therefore, behold, I will bring evil upon the house of Jeroboam, and will cut off from Jeroboam him that pisseth against the wall . . . and will take away the remnant of the house of Jeroboam, as a man taketh away dung, till it be all gone.' That was a God I understood; like the house of Jeroboam, I was being punished for my sins.

As miserable as I felt, I was free. I wasn't picking fights at literary parties across the river anymore. Single and broke gave me a different Williamsburg, the Williamsburg of Kokie's Place and the waterfront. Kokie's wasn't a bar for the stable, soon-to-be-married couple. You didn't spend hours wandering around the waterfront when you had a standing dinner date at home. When you had a home. My apartment was colder without Rebecca—I couldn't afford to turn on the heat. In the bathroom, I let the shower run hot for ten minutes—hot water was free—before I stripped down and shivered in. On the coldest nights, the shampoo froze in the bottle. It was hard to believe that we'd planned to be newlyweds there.

December 1994

'I love it!' Rebecca whispered as we nuzzled in the bathroom. Behind us in the hall the fat Polish landlady droned the enticements of the apartment—five forty a month, utilities included, newly painted, a block from the subway. She didn't mention that it was a hovel. That we could see for ourselves. The new paint stained our fingers and shoes.

I'd known Rebecca for five months and we'd been dating for two but there we were, lovers looking for a home. Rebecca (not her real name) was witty, she was beautiful, she was a talented poet, she thought I was a great writer: what more could a man want? We talked at speed, rattling over culture, art and the quirks of our friends. Rebecca said: 'You're the first guy I've dated who's as smart as I am.' (We were cocky too.) Nobody I knew in New York had an entire floor, with windows on both sides looking out on quiet yards. So what if the kitchen lacked a sink? All the way back to the realty office we decorated the place—her desk would be in the bedroom, mine in the living room. We could take breaks in bed and read our drafts to each other naked and warm. The shack would be our artists' colony. We'd be married too. First chance we had, we were going make a quick trip to Brooklyn Borough Hall; it was all so easy.

When I told Rose I was leaving, she threw a book at my head.

First and last—no security deposit—and Rebecca and I moved into 147 North Eighth Street RH ('rear house') a few days before the new year of 1995. The quiet rage of a blizzard emptied the streets and her car fishtailed down Union Avenue. The snow-muffled streets celebrated with us.

The apartment was on the first floor of a wood-frame house one block from the Bedford L station and two blocks from the river. On a good day you could be at Union Square in ten minutes, although a half hour jerking and starting between stations was the norm. The rent? Even I could come up with $270 a month. The floors slanted and the thresholds looked like they'd been carved by a drunk with a chain saw but somehow that made it even better. For weeks, the paint stayed wet and smeared our clothes because the landlady hadn't turned on the heat.

Like the Domino Sugar refinery, our cottage was a fragment of industrial Williamsburg: worker housing, the title deed dated 1905. In the 1930s a five-story apartment building had been squeezed onto the front of the long, narrow lot, leaving us at the back of a concrete courtyard. Our shack showed its age: when we turned on an air conditioner one night, fuses blew and the house went dark. An electrical fire in the subbasement was extinguished by a fortuitous flood (I didn't know there'd been a fire until I went to the basement and saw scorch marks on the wall). Then there was the day when we came home to the stench of natural gas. The gas line from the front house to our (illegal) wall heater had cracked, venting fuel. The pilot light was burning. A few more minutes and there would have been a crater in the middle of the block. The landlady had installed the heater herself and for months she told us that she was having nightmares about explosions. She didn't put in a new heater, though; a guilty conscience was cheaper. After that, we avoided temperature intervention, freezing in winter and melting in summer.

We loved the wild grapevines that grew along the walls and fences. We loved the rustic quiet; in deep night I could hear the subway roar in its burrow below the street. All sooty brick and vinyl siding, the Northside had been a factory ghetto for so long that it lacked the residue of gentility you saw in Fort Greene and Bed-Stuy, the Henry Jamesian mansions that made you ask, 'How did they ever let this place turn into a slum?' You didn't say the Northside was 'charming' or 'architecturally significant'; what you said was: 'It's so close to the city and so cheap!' Not long before we moved in, a fire burned through a row of tenements a few blocks north. A *Times* article about the fire labeled the neighborhood:

> . . . a working-class community with a large population of Polish and Hispanic immigrants, a district of tenement buildings, smoky factories and rundown warehouses that is known for environmental hazards and ranks highest in the city for leukemia in children and other cancers in adults.

The *Times* couldn't see the magic in the smoky factories and run-down warehouses. If Williamsburg had been its 1960s self—a thriving factory town—we would never have moved there. Roughneck teens talking shit on the corners, blue-collar bars, trucks jamming the streets, light rail on Metropolitan . . . There wouldn't have been space for us. The *Times* looked at Williamsburg and saw ruin; I looked at it and fell in love.

Rebecca started working at a Midtown literary agency and I watered plants, professionally. Two days a week, I got up at six a.m., caught the L and ran between Midtown and Wall Street with a watering can keeping *Ficus benjamina* and *Epipremnum aureum* (devil's ivy) alive in airline offices, investment banks and a Mercedes dealership. The gig paid just enough to make my end of the rent and bought me time to write. Writing was all that Rebecca and I wanted to do.

Playing the game, we went to Manhattan parties for young literary strivers. At one rooftop party, a sub-sub *New Yorker* editor asked us where we lived.

Oh, Williamsburg, he said. Places there are pretty cheap, right?

He leaned over, his knit tie brushing a small mound of cocaine on top of a central-air unit. He hoovered a line.

Of course, he said, why come to New York if you're not going to live in Manhattan? That's the whole point, right?

I guess, I said.

Later he asked me if I read the magazine.

Sure, I said. *The New Yorker* has great articles. But the fiction is mostly crap. What do you work on there?

Fiction, he said.

By 1995 you could walk home from the L at night and not get jumped by a crackhead. Bedford Avenue pulsed with immigrant vigor: a Polish bakery, a Polish pharmacy, two Polish butchers two doors apart, three Polish restaurants and a Polish florist, the flowers overpriced and wilted (I walked by for years but never saw a customer inside; it all seemed very shady). Even the Puerto Rican bodegas sold Żywiec and Warka, and Poles were buying buildings and becoming landlords. The Polish beachhead met Williamsburg past and Williamsburg to come: a Russian-owned hardware store, a card shop, three bars—Muggs, the Charlestown and the Greenpoint Tavern—and six bodegas, three owned by a feuding Palestinian family.

Rebecca and I had found our apartment through Kenn Firpo, the one Northside Realtor. His tiny office was right around the corner on Bedford. The plaster-smeared walls and battered desk made it seem like he'd set up shop the day before and would disappear in the night one step ahead of creditors and cops. Large and hirsute, Firpo looked like he would happily crack the kneecaps of deadbeat lessees. Old paperbacks lined office shelves; the Northside Realtor was also a used-book dealer. Then there was the L Café, the Northside's living room.

The café is gentrification's trading post, where under-employed artists stare into mud and dream of masterpieces.* Now that cafés have become a strip-mall standard it's hard to remember how unnatural they were in this country not so long ago. A place where people sit for hours, not spending money or making it, goes against the American grain. In an industrial town like Williamsburg, opening a café didn't occur to the native. Sure, there were cafés on the other side of the BQE, Old World holdovers where Italian grandfathers gossiped and complained over espressos. The L Café was something new, a sign of climate change sweeping out from the Lower East Side.

In the back of the café next to the bathrooms a cork board listed apartments, performances, junk for sale and bands looking for a 'drummer. Our influences: Rush, Moby Grape, Hank Williams. Chops a plus but attitude more important. No big hair.' The vacant storefront next to the L served similar fare, boards over the windows fliered in soft layers inches deep. There was no Craigslist and no Wi-Fi; the L collated us.

The L's long decline and fall, the fast-forward changes in everything Williamsburg, efface how central the café was to the neighborhood. During rushes, a human python twisted down the aisles and out the door. If Rebecca and I

---

*The café precedes the bookstore but the bookstore is always on the minds of culture-starved settlers. No fewer than five people came up to me in Williamsburg before 2000 and said, 'Hey, man, we should open a bookstore!' (Firpo's two shelves of battered paperbacks didn't qualify.)

landed a table on Sunday morning, we felt like lottery winners. We'd drop all four hundred pounds of the *Times* on the table and dicker over favored sections—book review, week in review, arts, magazine. The sports page was all mine.

In the years after college I'd struggled to write a novel and published a few book reviews, but I wasn't discouraged. Writing was my religion. It was why I had a clown job and scraped along on $800 a month. Writing was also boring. That's why there aren't any good movies about writing, why so many talented people who want to write can't do it. The boredom breaks them. If you don't have bipolar disorder like Dickens you turn to coffee and Benzedrine, Adderall and kratom. Cafés are a way to cheat the boredom. A flatmate in San Francisco had started me on the path—I think he was sick of me always being in the house. 'You should try writing in a café,' Wolfgang said. He even told me where to go, the International on lower Haight. (As a suave, gay German, he went to Café Flore, a place for the gay and suave.) Wolfgang was right—in the café you found noise, movement, people to flirt with. An asshole critic for the *New York Press* published a column berating café writers. We were pretentious. We were showing off. We were wasting time. True enough, but so what? For me, the café made the boredom easier to take.

An agent at Rebecca's agency read my novel and decided to represent me. I finally had an excuse for all the wasted time.

L Café coffee was toxic but the cup was bottomless and two dollars meant I could sit and watch the neighborhood. I got to know my fellow travelers, artists in their twenties and thirties trying to make something out of nothing. A filmmaker who punched me in the face the first time we met. A lawyer who'd bailed on his profession to become a screenwriter. ('Patent law,' he said. 'Just imagine reading your toaster warranty all day long.') A bearded painter from Iowa whose favorite subjects were boxers, bulldogs and cheerleaders and who drank like a football frat.

Other faces clarified from the blur. A beautiful woman with green animal eyes who Rebecca dubbed 'Wolf Girl.' A plump fortune-teller layered in skirts and mascara who went from table to table clutching palms (she told me I had two love lines and no life line). A tense, sweating Thai whose only English seemed to be 'Tiger's Balm' and 'two dollar' as he smiled and showed you the tin. Then there was a bum who sprawled without shame against the café storefront on warm days. Sores and scabs marred his naked legs and serous fluid glistened on his shins.

I been dead three times, Frank the Bum told us at the café counter after another hospital sojourn. Gauze swathed his head and his eyes were deleted, as if rough thumbs had popped them free and we looked into all the darkness of skull. Frank detested the café owner but cold weather overcame his principles.

This last time, Frank said, I woke up with a syringe in my chest. I asked the doctor, 'What are you doing?' He said, 'You had no vital signs. We had to give you the injection.' I told him: 'The next time I wake up with a syringe in my chest, I'm gonna stick it in your eyeball.' What have I got to live for?

It was a rhetorical question, one with no comfortable answer, as Frank was homeless on the streets where he'd once swaggered. I will not hesitate to name Frank 'bum' in these pages since that's what he called himself, and his defensive pride strikes me as more honest than any euphemism, his kingdom the strip of sidewalk extending from the bodega on Bedford and North Seventh to the door of the L Café itself, his royal bed wherever he could make it.

There was also a soft-spoken local with copper skin, gangster vines and waist-length dreads. His reserve made him an anti-Frank. Every night around closing he walked in and sipped espresso as chairs were lifted to tabletops. A waitress told me his name was Napoleon.

Napoleon

As the L train barreled along the Fourteenth Street tunnel, Napoleon turned to his friend.

We're not going to Lorimer, he said. Let's get off at Bedford and see what's going on.

Napoleon had noticed a change in the L at the First Avenue stop: all the white people didn't get off. Poles had always gone through to Bedford but one day a punk rocker stayed on the train. Then Napoleon saw more white guys in paint-splattered overalls do the same. The new faces tended to congregate in the last car.

I kind of asked myself, Napoleon says, 'What are you doing in the neighborhood?' I didn't know. One, two, three, four gradually became like ten in the car. Then twenty.

The Lorimer L stop at Union and Metropolitan marked a division: west of Union and south of Grand you entered a Hispanic world. The other compass points brought you to an Italian neighborhood aging and shrinking away from its old boundaries. Napoleon usually walked west from the Lorimer stop back to his home on South Second. That day, though, he followed the 'artistic' people out of the station at Bedford Avenue. Though he lived only ten blocks away, Napoleon hadn't been on the Northside for years.

We get out, start walking around, Napoleon says. I see Planet Thailand. Okay. I see L Café. I see Veracruz. Mind you, before this the Northside was completely boarded up. Dead. A wasteland. And now you had these little stores.

They passed a Bedford Avenue storefront that had been cleaned, repainted peach and filled with junk from some antebellum grandfather's basement. It looked like a Catskills yard sale, down to the old dressers and tables stacked on the sidewalk. That was Ugly Luggage.

Napoleon was intrigued enough to go back to the Northside a few days later with the same friend. They ended up at the L Café. After an awkward wait they took a table—waiters didn't show you to your seats, they weren't your *slaves*—and ordered coffee. Napoleon and his friend sat and talked. And sat and talked. For hours. Nobody kicked them out, even though they weren't spending five dollars between the two of them. In fact, the waiter kept bringing more coffee.

It was great, Napoleon says. But it was also kind of sad. No one spoke to me. Except the waiter. 'May I take your order? Cup of coffee? Would you like anything else?' And that's it.

Other customers greeted the waiter by name. They had long conversations, the waiter leaning against the wall. The guy working the counter shared jokes with regulars. New customers came in and hollered, 'What's up?' to the whole room.

I started thinking, Napoleon says, 'I'm going to be like that.' And I told my friend . . . I was like, 'See that guy over there? That girl? I'm going to be like that when I come in. Watch. Just give me some time.'

Napoleon was Southside Dominican all the way. His parents had come to the States in the early seventies on a

Caribbean tsunami a hundred feet high. Napoleon's enormous family—his great-grandmother had twenty-four kids—flowed between New York and Santo Domingo. When they went to Coney Island or the Rockaways in the summer, they made their own traffic jam.

It wasn't two cars, Napoleon says. It was seventeen cars. I remember seeing lines of cars, cars, cars. Everybody was just jammed in. There'd be an old Nova or something with eight people hanging out of it. Like a clown car.

Mostly his family worked in construction or in garment sweatshops as seamstresses, pattern makers and pressers. When garment work shifted to Asia and Mexico and the local sweatshops shut down, they found work as home attendants and car service drivers, or they opened small businesses (Napoleon's mother had a clothing boutique). Napoleon lived on Havemeyer and South Third until he was seven and his family moved to South Second between Keap and Hooper. His extended family occupied dozens of apartments in the area, making the streets between Grand and South Fourth a vast and comfortable front yard.

In his Southside enclave, Napoleon was closer to Hispaniola than to Manhattan. His parents spoke Spanish at home and sent him to their village in the DR every summer. By the time he came back to P.S. 84, he had forgotten his English and his teachers tried to transfer him to remedial classes.

That was one of my nightmares, Napoleon says. Oh, no, they're going to put me in bilingual school. 'I know English,' I'd tell them. 'I was born here.'

Bringing English books and tapes with him on vacation solved the language problem but it didn't take care of his cultural confusion. He wasn't Dominican to Dominicans or American to his grade school teachers. To Southside Puerto

Ricans he was undoubtedly Dominican, which made him the enemy. Coming home from school when he was seven, he had to run a gauntlet of older Puerto Rican kids with a question: Puerto Rican or Dominican?

I told them I was Dominican, Napoleon says. I felt this pride and I couldn't lie. And they were like, 'Ohhhh. Ohhhh.' I said, 'What are you gonna do? Beat me up for it?' I started talking in Spanish and they got a little embarrassed. Because a lot of the Puerto Ricans here don't even speak Spanish.

He was caught in the kids' version of the turf wars shaking the Southside as Dominican newcomers battled with Puerto Ricans over the drug corners, as heroin's long reign was threatened by coke, and junkies with steady habits gave way to desperate crackheads. In years to come, Napoleon would see certain of his cousins get involved in everything from machete fights on school playgrounds to drive-by shootings.

With his English under control, Napoleon found himself in honors classes. His main interest was drawing and sketching; Napoleon was the kid whose art pinned by the refrigerator magnet actually impresses someone besides Mom. 'He's gonna be an artist,' Napoleon's mother would say. 'A painter or something.' For junior high he transferred into an accelerated program at the Manhattan Academy of Technology, Jacob Riis, P.S. 126, taking the L into the city every morning. Jacob Riis was full of nerds; on the Southside, nerds got their glasses broken.

Kids will test you on the Southside, Napoleon says. They'll slap you in the back of the head. If you let it slide, guess what? Fourteen other guys want to slap you in the back of the head. And what are you gonna do after three or four of them do it? You gonna start with the first guy who did it or the last guy? Or the next nine guys who are gonna slap you? I was the quiet dude, so a lot of times guys would come up and I had to show them it was the wrong move.

Meanwhile, Napoleon's friends from grammar school were back at John D. Wells Junior High on South Third and Driggs having the time of their lives, or at least that's how they sold it to Napoleon.

They told me, he says, 'We're having a blast. We're wrestling, we're having water balloon fights in school, we're cutting out of class and just leaving.' They made it seem like paradise. So I self-sabotaged.

Napoleon stopped doing homework. He missed classes. He didn't turn in his reports. Sure enough, he washed out of 126 and transferred to John D. Wells in time for the eighth grade. His test scores still put him in honors classes so he only hung out with his friends at lunch and after school, which was enough. Napoleon planned to send his portfolio to the High School of Art and Design in Midtown but missed the deadline after breaking his leg in a basketball game. So for his freshman year in 1987, he ended up at Eli Whitney on North Sixth and Havemeyer: a bad school in a bad neighborhood. Whores paraded along that block night and day and in a mixture of lust, curiosity and contempt, kids would shout at them from behind the safety of the fence. Napoleon remembers the corner being so rough that he planned his route home to avoid it.

At Eli Whitney, Napoleon studied woodworking, carpentry and industrial design.

It's not what I wanted to learn, he says. So I started cutting classes and hanging out.

By 1987, thousands of Dominicans lived on the Southside. 'In factories—Dominicans. Restaurants—Dominicans. In clubs—the Dominicans. Then the streets—Dominicans.'

Napoleon noticed that the roughest guys, the real gangsters, came from Santo Domingo.

They came hungry, Napoleon says. They were like, 'We're gonna make ours here.'

They'd brought their connections with them, and gangs and drugs brought danger. When Napoleon left his house, he'd always check the street to see if it was clear.

You never know, Napoleon says, who'd show up being chased by the guys from the Borinquen projects or the Marcy projects or whatever beef came along the way.

Often it was Napoleon's friends being chased. They'd bonded for years but that didn't mean Napoleon knew what had them running down Grand Street in the middle of the afternoon. Had they stolen a car? Shot somebody? He had no idea. One night he was standing on the corner of South Second and Havemeyer when somebody said, 'That's the fourth time that car with tinted windows went by. Look out.'

All of a sudden, boom, boom, boom—it's a shootout, Napoleon says. I'm ducking. I'm falling on the ground real quick. I'm going home. I was down with those guys but not like that. People were always trying to recruit me: 'You want to be down with this posse? You want to be down with my crew?' I was like, 'No. I'm my own self.' I had a lot of friends who did that. Some of them are in jail now.

By Napoleon's junior year at Whitney, the guidance counselor had seen enough. He called Napoleon into his office and told him that he should consider dropping out.

That surprised me, Napoleon says. I was like, 'Whoa, you're my guidance counselor, why are you telling me to drop out?' And he said, 'Because I know you're smart. And because I dropped out, got my GED and went to college.'

A week later, Napoleon took the counselor's advice. No more morning marches down Havemeyer to woodshop purgatory. College would have to wait, though, while Napoleon went into business on the Southside.

Rebecca and I never made it to Borough Hall. I can still see her sitting in the L wearing her grandmother's white mink coat, see the thick black curls that corkscrewed over her shoulders framing her green eyes and creamy skin. If I left the table for five minutes, some art-school alley cat would be on her, saying, 'So you're a writer. What are you working on?' I don't know what makes relationships last but I know all the ways they can go wrong. I can still hear Rebecca yelling and pounding on the bathroom door as I sat on the toilet lid and plugged my ears.

The Irish Catholic cannibal and the Jewish dentist's daughter were not compatible. That was our failing, but Williamsburg played a supporting role in the wreck. Rebecca loved the Northside, but her friends lived on West End Avenue and in Yorkville and SoHo. They had parents' money and parents' expectations. They went to law school if the art thing didn't work out. Except for the money—a big 'except'—being privileged seemed like a drag. Me, as long as I had time to write, I was happy with the watering can. Expectations meant that Rebecca tried to do everything—work a forty-hour week at the literary agency, go to grad school full-time, run a reading series at Alt.Coffee on Avenue A. She was smart—smart!—and she had a soul. But she'd never been adrift. She had a tether. Most of the people I got to know in Williamsburg didn't. We were drifting. When Rebecca left I did something I hadn't done in almost a decade—I cried, after clamping a pillow to my face so that nobody could hear me.

We didn't stay in touch. Twelve years later, she published a novel about the Northside. I saw our apartment through the eyes of a ghost. "They lived where they could afford to live without the dreaded parental supplementation: in run-down tenements on narrow Brooklyn blocks, illegal sublets found through friends of friends (who could afford a broker's fee?), or rickety apartments in crumbling back-houses, let by landlords who'd never heard the word 'code' in their miserly lives . . ." A Williamsburg novel from someone who lived there eleven months said something about the neighborhood in 1995: even passing through you felt the allure.

Marcin

Hammering brought me out of my apartment, the building flapping like a billboard in a hurricane. Downstairs a slender dark-haired man was banging away at his front door.

Hello, he said, presenting a hammer. I am putting on new lock.

The landlady had lost the spare key to his rooms below the stairs. In the future a padlock would hang there, making it look like a stable for a goat, not a home for a man.

You're Robert, he said in accented English. You live upstairs.

I walked down and gripped a soft hand.

My name is Marcin, he said. It sounded like 'Martian.'

He was in his mid-twenties, a few inches taller than me but he stooped. Fine dark hair that he obviously cut himself fell over his forehead. His eyes were dark too, deep brown irises merging with shrunken pupils.

Your girlfriend moved out, he said.

Yes, she did, I said. He'd probably heard us fighting.

I've seen you around the neighborhood, he said.

That made me uneasy. I wondered where he'd seen me and what I'd been doing. Marcin had replaced another Pole, that one at least six-six and famine thin. I'd only known him from his midnight sessions on Fender Telecaster and the crates of empty beer bottles that appeared outside his door.

We talked for a while, made fun of the landlady and I went back up the stairs.

Takin' easy, Marcin said as I walked away.

I soon found out that Marcin was a photographer and an unrepentant junkie. Marcin's addiction and his photos came out of the same distorting blackness. He would become obsessed with people in the neighborhood and follow them, shooting from a distance. They never seemed to notice. He showed me photos he'd taken of me before we met. His theories for why I'd been in the places he'd shot me were generally wrong and often insane. When I told Marcin he was mistaken he'd smile and nod, as if to say that of course he understood why I was deceiving him.

On my way to a temp job one morning, I ran into Marcin in a subway car. He was so blasted on heroin that he couldn't speak, eyes and nose crusted with mucus. It was eight-thirty.

I'd find the landlady and Marcin gossiping on the stoop. Henryka distrusted Marcin as much as I did but that didn't keep her from repeating his stories. She'd stop me in the hallway or on the street and say, 'That girl you were with

last week—she is your new girlfriend? Marcin tell me this.'
'No,' I'd say. 'That was . . .' my sister, my cousin. My aunt. Mother Teresa. 'Oh,' she said. 'But Marcin tell me that you have very many girls here.'

You can't trust Marcin, I said. He's a Gypsy.

She cackled at that: thirty years in New York but still in a Polish village, and Marcin's shiftiness exactly evoked 'Gypsy' to her shrewd, paranoid, bigoted Eastern European mind.

I'd been surprised that the landlady had rented the basement to Marcin in the first place. When Rebecca and I moved in, the building was solidly Polish except for a guy who'd been in the Dictators and two women, flatmates, that I'd gone to college with. An older Polish couple lived in the apartment above ours with their twentysomething nephew (when his aunt and uncle relocated to Greenpoint the nephew came out as gay and hosted all-night parties to frenetic house beats). Whenever Poles moved out the landlady replaced them with young Americans. I asked Henryka why and she said: 'No more Polish. Polish too much drink.' It wasn't a lie—by eight o'clock on Friday night there was always at least one middle-aged Polish man in the Bedford Avenue gutter. Still, I thought 'not enough money' mattered more to the landlady than 'too much drink.' Marcin had gotten the apartment because Henryka hadn't registered it with the city. She was a shrewd businesswoman and understood that a Polish junkie on a dubious visa meant less potential for legal trouble than an American kid with professional parents.

Like Ying and Rose, Marcin didn't fit into the world. Not quite Polish, not quite an artist. But he shared his Williamsburg with me. From Marcin I learned that Raymund's Place on Bedford and North Eleventh had the best Polish food and that SUV-driving Hasidic men kept the Kent Avenue hookers in business.

Marcin's apartment made mine look like Lee Iacocca's suite at the Waldorf. He had lacquered the floors though and was replacing the old floorboards one at a time. Through rectangular gaps, I could see into the flooded subbasement with its dirt foundation. Palmetto bugs (*Periplaneta americana*) scuttled through his two rooms. The six-foot tinplate ceiling stopped inches short of Marcin's scalp. When we hung out there, Marcin would do lines of dope off the top of the *Alien Lanes* CD I'd loaned him.

The Devil and the East River

New York is crowded. Other people always get in your way. You can't stretch your legs without kicking somebody and you can't think without static from 8 million other brains. If you can't afford quiet space you take it where you can get it, in a park or in a library, or you rent it for a few hours in movie-theater dark. But the library closes and the movie ends. In the decades before I came to New York people had left cities by the hundreds of thousands, something that hadn't happened in the Western world since the Black Death. That exodus brought the frontier to Williamsburg, and one thing the frontier has is plenty of space.

It wasn't named for coke, the bartender said. That's the funny thing. I mean, the place opened in the fifties and it sure wasn't pushing coke back then.

The bartender was thick—thick torso, thick neck, thick skin, fingers like cannolis and that blunt Long Island accent, Brooklynese tempered by a generation in the suburbs. But he could tell a story.

They got this frog in Puerto Rico, he said. It's called a coqui because of the sound it makes: 'ko-kee, ko-kee, ko-kee.' The guy who owned this place was Puerto Rican. Back then, it was some kind of social club. He used to have card games in here, strippers, that kind of thing. I mean he was half a wiseguy anyway. One night he got stabbed in a card game. That was it for him. He was like, 'I'm seventy years old. I don't need this shit.' So he gave the place to his nephew and *that's* when it got started. One of the old doormen comes in here and we talk.

The Antique Lounge had opened a couple of months earlier at the end of 2002. Its antique flourishes came courtesy of a restaurant catalog—tin ceiling, exposed brick, classic moldings and a fireplace. The furniture was quicksand plush: you sank right in. Nothing was left from the long reign of Kokie's.

I'm forty-three years old, the bartender said. I'm in it for the long haul. This place is my dream. I was born in the neighborhood. When I was four my parents moved out to Lynbrook but we stayed connected.

The bartender was also the owner. Blond salon streaks in his hair and his padded face made him look younger.

The Kokie's crew had a great take in here, he said. Twenty thousand dollars for a four-day week. That's not bad—even if you include the coke. Of course, you don't know how many people were getting envelopes. After 9/11 that all changed. Well, the city changed but they didn't. Everything stayed right out in the open. I mean, if you're gonna do that, at least be discreet. But no. They had the salsa band in here. The noise at seven a.m. Still, they never got busted. That's the funny thing. They lost their lease first. They got some kind of three-strikes thing in New York, I don't know the legal particulars but the landlord was afraid they'd take away his building. So he didn't renew the lease.*

The owner bought me a drink. The way he talked, I figured that he'd been a Kokie's customer himself.

The neighbors hated them more than anything, he said. When I took over they came in to check us out. When I told them what I was doing, they thanked me. You know, the Kokie's crew thought they were being discreet. That's the funny thing. With the booths in the back and leaning against the wall to put in your order. And the way they used to cut that stuff to shit. Why not have a decent product? But they really stepped on it. What went on with Kokie's, I couldn't have that. Most of my family is cops so . . .

We looked around the quiet lounge—five or six people submerged in the couches and sofas, classic rock playing on the jukebox. We could have been in any of fifty New York City bars. 'Antique' was in.

We did all our own renovations. We soundproofed the ceiling. We put in our own hot water—the guy upstairs used to share it. And it's working out. Couples like it here. We got the couches. It's romantic. Last week we had fifty dykes for a party. Not too many of them were those lipstick lesbians, I tell you. But nice people. Polite. That's the kind of place I want. The guy who owns Rain came in here last week. You know what he told me?

Rain Lounge had opened the year before on Bedford and North Fifth. The 'urban' vibe made it an anomaly even

*In a different take on the end of Kokie's, *VICE* magazine reports one 'Rick P.' as saying: "The final nail in the coffin came when the local precinct got a new police captain who had come straight from doing narcotics and vice work. She wasn't having a coke bar in her precinct. They busted the place a few times and that's pretty much the end of the story."

on a changing Northside—flash cars parked in front, gangster vines, hip-hop thumping, meaty bouncers. The fact that both longtime locals and newcomers disdained the only neighborhood club that catered to African Americans said something about tolerance for 'diversity.'

He told me, the bartender said, 'I dread going to work. The fights. The girls passed out on E. The guns.' I told him, 'You don't have to do it.' But he said no. That's the choice he made. He probably takes in thirty-five hundred on a Friday night. Me, I'm doing good if I get that in a week. Then again, he's probably paying eight grand a month for that corner. I pay twenty-five hundred. The authorities have it out for him too. I had the fire inspectors in here, the safety marshals. They told me, 'We got the inspection list for Rain. We're going to nail them for this and this and this.' That's not the crowd I want. I won't play hip-hop or techno. I'm in it for the long haul.

I went back to the Antique Lounge a few times after that to commune with the ghosts of Kokie's, but the bar had nothing for me. By the next winter, the Antique Lounge had closed and Rain wasn't too far behind. Kokie's business model beat theirs by almost half a century.

The Priceless Gem

In 1987, fifty-seven-year-old Harry Havemeyer took a melancholy drive along the Williamsburg waterfront. To Harry, the patchwork of shuttered factories, empty streets and jungle lots was particularly grim: he knew he was looking at the ruins of an empire.

He knew because he came from the royal family. 'Harry'

was Henry William Havemeyer, scion of Domino Sugar. His great-grandfather William Havemeyer had opened a sugar refinery on Vandam Street in Manhattan in 1807 and by the end of the century the 'sugar trust' under Henry Osborne Havemeyer controlled 98 percent of the refined sugar produced in the United States. The Havemeyers also owned almost every lot on the Williamsburg waterfront between South Fifth and North Tenth Streets. 'Their fascination with real estate,' Harry wrote, 'led them to believe that real estate, rather than sugar, was the priceless gem to be retained in the family.'

For over a century the five black arts—glassmaking, pottery making, printing, refining and cast-iron manufacture—dosed Williamsburg air and water and soil. With its santonin, citric acid and penicillin, Pfizer made another kind of dark magic in a fifteen-acre compound on Flushing Avenue at the neighborhood's southern verge. Sugar built the castles, though; sugar stoked immigration until a village nestled on the edge of the East River became the most densely populated town in the United States. Post–Civil War America burned west on Williamsburg sugar. In H. O. Havemeyer, Williamsburg had a robber baron out of central casting—Henry even had a moustache to stroke as he bought politicians and spilled blood on the cobblestones of Kent Street when he had police shoot striking refinery workers. The Spanish-American War is sometimes called 'Havemeyer's War' because he promoted it as a shortcut to buying Cuban sugar plantations.

Refined sugar was America's drug of choice, one that didn't have to worry about the Untouchables, or that 'bulldog running along at the feet of Jesus,' Carrie Nation. Bubble Yum and Coca-Cola and everything Hostess propelled my brothers and me through childhood. Our nickels, dimes and quarters kept the corner stores in business (I remember the glorious day I discovered Chocodiles, and how they still cost only a quarter into my stoner teens). Even our break-fast cereal came with a factory-appliquéd white crust. My mother managed to resist our sugar lust just enough to hold us to one box of sugar cereal a week each. Having to choose was almost unbearable, there were so many delicious op-tions: Sugar Frosted Flakes and Sugar Corn Pops and Sugar Smacks and Super Sugar Crisp, Cap'n Crunch's Peanut But-ter Crunch and Franken Berry, Cap'n Crunch's Crunch Ber-ries and the short-lived but greatly missed (by me)—Jean LaFoote's Cinnamon Crunch. Since a box could go in a day, we hunted through the house to raid each other's stash. The dentist's drill whined. 'Kids' teeth are just cavity-prone,' he said.

Harry Havemeyer's melancholy tour didn't stop at Kokie's and he doesn't mention the bar. Yet its influence was every-where. Mounds of white crystals rose on kitchen tables across Williamsburg, Bed-Stuy, Brownsville and Washing-ton Heights. Every crystal mound had started out as a flow-ering plant, hundreds of acres of them, thousands of miles to the south. Crushed and processed, the plants shrank and lost color—green to brown to yellow to glittering white. What they lost in color they gained in power, energy con-centrated until it could ignite cells and shift bodies at car-toon speeds. Fossil fuel, that black blood of the earth, drove every step of the transformation. By the 1950s, the sugar barons had lost their hold on Williamsburg. H. O. Have-meyer had reigned with a legitimacy that Cali cartel bosses could only envy, but their product ruled the decaying streets. Like the five-and-dimes where my brothers and I scored

Charleston Chews, Kokie's retailed cheap thrills. I careened around the dance floor like I had around the breakfast table on Lorimer Avenue.

I soon figured out how Kokie's operated. There was no point in going there before two in the morning, when bars like Muggs and the Greenpoint Tavern emptied. You went to Kokie's on nights when everything was right or everything was wrong and you couldn't bear to go home. The zombie ogre with the mop was the guy who got the coke for you (or the DJ did). You'd lean against a wall next to the DJ booth, wait for one of them to come over and pass him the cash. A few minutes later he'd amble back and palm you a packet. Bouncers hustled people in and out of the booths so quickly that you'd wind up doing key bumps with complete strangers. I learned that the product at Kokie's burned like Ajax and shook you like the Coney Island Cyclone. Whatever went into the cut—plaster dust, chalk, aspirin, Pez?—my joke was that they weren't doing anything illegal since their shit couldn't possibly be coke.

I spent my share of too-late nights there, nights initiated when someone at a party would bellow 'Let's go to Kokie's!' We were young and sick with energy, not ready to give up on a night that was almost morning. We wanted to stop time. I found out that you could do your coke in a bathroom stall if the line for the booths was long. I learned that the people I knew from daytime Williamsburg were different when you met them in the night swirl of Kokie's.

At the end of a too-long New Year's Eve, I brought a Brit musician to the bar. Spenser's claim to fame was a stint in the Smiths (he'd been kicked out for too much partying). As we swilled more liquor we didn't need, a fight broke out and holiday suits and gowns tumbled around the room. Thirty-five seconds later, cops showed up and settled everything down. The bartender slapped the cops on the back and called them by name. As we left, Spenser kept shaking his head.

If there was a bar in hell, he said, it would be Kokie's.

Hell made for good company: I met all kinds of people in the camaraderie of intoxication—musicians, thugs, stockbrokers, late-shift workers from a nearby factory that made polyethylene bags. I remember talking one night to a local kielbasa maker, a man as square and red as a new brick. He introduced himself as Pat Driscoll.

Yeah, I'm a butcher, he said. Sausage. I'm very good with the smoked meats.

Driscoll reached into his overcoat and pulled out a golden disc with a pig embossed it and the words 'First Place.'

I got this last week at a big meat product competition, he said. In Wisconsin. Second year in a row. It's the first time I've been out of town in five years. I'm from Greenpoint.

So you must be Polish, I said.

No, he said. That's the funny thing. It's all Polish now but not when I was growing up. I'm half Irish, half Italian. All the stores up there are Polish. Most of my friends left years ago. Where do I fit in? I want to move away but I'm stuck here. Where else do they need a sausage maker? Chicago? There's a lot of Poles in Chicago who can do my job.

In the glow from the drug we were the best of friends, so I tried to cheer him up.

Well, I said, only Brooklyn has Kokie's.

I've been coming to Kokie's for twenty-five years, he said. It's changed a lot too. Used to be all Spanish but look at it now.

His arm swept the room, taking in the salsa band, the middle-aged Hispanic women with hennaed hair stepping lightly and the skinny hipster boys staggering around like they were on an obstacle course. Bodies jittered out of the back booths and turned into people I knew—local musicians, bodega clerks, a porcine gallery owner groping women who weren't his wife.

Kokie's was the Bella Union Saloon of an urban Deadwood. And there was frontier violence. People got attacked walking through the deserted streets. A friend of mine woke up in the local precinct house covered in blood. The police guessed that he'd been hit with a baseball bat. The last thing he remembered was saying goodnight to the bouncer at Kokie's.

Esther Bell

A gunshot and the crunch of steel woke up Esther in the predawn gray. From her window she saw a car askew across Berry on North Third. A crumpled fender and the gouged chassis of parked cars showed the path the town car had taken. Esther noticed a figure behind the wheel. It didn't move. Soon cops arrived to direct traffic and string yellow tape. Whatever had happened, Esther was pretty sure it had something to do with her neighbor three floors below.

In 1996, Esther moved to Williamsburg from the Lower East Side. Rising rent and a breakup sent her east but those weren't the only reasons. One night on Avenue A she'd come home to find a woman unconscious in her doorway.

I walked over her without blinking an eye, Esther says. Assuming she was another heroin addict. That made me realize I needed to go somewhere else. I just couldn't believe that it was me that felt normal walking over practically dead people at my door.

Esther schlepped most of the nothing she owned on the

L train. 'Which took like an hour in those days,' she says. On her last transit she carried a houseplant. The houseplant's name was Billy.

I was walking down Bedford, Esther says, and there were no shops or anything. But this Polish woman came up to me and started talking about my plant. I told her that I named it 'Billy' for 'Billyburg,' and she thought that was really funny and she said, 'Well, welcome to the neighborhood.' And I thought, 'Wow, I've really entered an entirely different world here.'

Eight years of hopping around Manhattan and no stranger had ever welcomed her to a new home.

Esther took the lease from the sister of a friend. The woman was pregnant and had decided that infant + coke bar = terrible mother. Esther remembers the woman warning her: 'Maybe you don't want to hang out downstairs.' The Northside wasn't exactly Mayberry but the apartment was big—big living room, big bedroom, kitchen—and it only cost $600 a month. Esther could live alone, finally, and could sublet the place in a minute when she was traveling to make her film, a feature with locations in South Carolina. Life always had trade-offs; in New York they were just more extreme. She'd have to tough out the coke bar part.

In high school, Esther had picked up a Super 8 camera and started making short documentaries. One short about the Southern indie rock scene won an award from TBS, but that didn't inspire Esther to keep shooting. To her, documentaries weren't real movies. By the time she reached City College, she'd settled on a serious major—the ancient Near East. She'd kept the camera though. When her Lower East Side roommate introduced her to the designer Stephen Sprouse, they decided to make a series of experimental films. 'I shot all their beautiful junkie friends,' Esther says. 'It was like Warhol but instead of the Factory we had a three-hundred-square-foot loft.'

Esther got to hang out with Debbie Harry but, more important, she saw the camera as a way to make art. By the time she moved to Williamsburg, she hadn't thought about the ancient Near East in a long time.

Industry wasn't dead on the Northside and diesel rigs lined North Third through the night. After-hours clubs and truckers kept similar schedules. The truck stop also provided a marketplace for prostitutes.

Every time I walked down Berry Street, Esther says, I was solicited by Hasidic men or truckers because they thought I was a crack whore. I mean, I was actually pretty insulted that they couldn't tell the difference because I do like to eat and the crack whores don't, and they have bad fashion sense. So I was thinking, 'Wow, come on guys, get a clue.'

A photo Esther took from the window on the day of the shooting shows a gray town car—it's a black-and-white photo—tilted against a Jeep Wagoneer with tinted windows and those trademark wood-grain panels. The angle of the town car and the fact that it has two wheels on the sidewalk suggests collision. An ambulance blocks the street. Uniformed men stand in small groups. The town car stayed in the street all afternoon, corpse languishing at the wheel. Esther worked on her taxes and took window breaks but she didn't want to go outside.

Late in the day a police detective buzzed Esther's door and came upstairs. He told Esther that a car service driver had been shot in the head while idling in front of the bar. His foot had pressed the gas pedal and sailed the car across Berry.

Oh, Esther said, I guess the murder probably has some-thing to do with the bar downstairs.

Oh, no, the detective said. No. I don't think so.

No one was ever charged with the murder.

Esther's landlord was an ex-cop and rumor had it that his brother was the local precinct captain. The landlord didn't make any repairs in her apartment—even though an enormous hole in her bathroom floor gaped down on the stairwell—but he did give Esther a brief history of Kokie's. It had started out in the 1900s as an Italian social club. Then in the 1950s, as Puerto Ricans moved into Williamsburg, it turned into a Spanish club, complete with cockfights. When the grandson of the first Puerto Rican owner took over, the bar wasn't making any money from old-timers paying a dol-lar a beer so the grandson turned it into an after-hours club. He knew what he was doing. A local writer tells a story of going to Kokie's on Halloween and noticing the squad cars parked around the building. 'I thought, "That's it,"' he said. 'Somebody got shot or they got busted.' As he waited outside he saw costumed partyers leaving the bar in no particular hurry, so he went in. Eleven years later, what he saw still makes him shake his head. 'The entire staff,' he says. 'Bar-tenders, bouncer, DJ, *everyone*, was dressed as a cop. I guess they had a sense of humor.'

I'd be home for a quiet night of work when I'd get frantic, turn up the music and shake out of my skin. I'd have a beer and run into the street looking for contact, who, what, where almost didn't matter. I spent more late nights at Kokie's than I should have and I wasn't the only one: a Swedish painter told me he'd walked into Kokie's on a Thursday and didn't leave until Sunday morning (except for a short break to cook ketamine on someone's stove). We had too much energy and Kokie's helped to burn it away. Energy had brought us to Williamsburg and our energy was changing the neighborhood. Energy had renovated Stephan's apartment and had me drinking coffee and trying to write at one a.m. when I had to get up at seven. Energy was taking an abandoned industrial neighborhood and reshaping it. Kokie's was only the last stop for the energy working on the storefronts and lofts and studios. Our energy had a particular valence, one that was outcompeting the Poles for space on the Northside.

It took a while before I got brave enough to go to Kokie's sober and alone. That's when I realized that Kokie's wasn't important because it was a place to get wasted, any more than the waterfront mattered as a place to tan. The world is full of places to get fucked-up, and the majority of them don't serve vodka tonics in Dixie cups. Kokie's and the waterfront were different in almost every way, but they both set us free. I'd hit Kokie's before a waterfront ramble or go to the bar to warm myself after the windy shore. As two feet of snow fell on Brooklyn one Saturday night, I went to Kokie's to find it closed, then tromped down to the water in my boots and stood on the bulkhead watching fat snowflakes dissolve in the East River. Eight million bodies out there and I could have been the only person in the world.

Down by the River

On a warm September day, Marcin knocked on my door.

Are you ready? he said.

The night before we'd been up late talking collaboration. There were stories in Williamsburg, we were sure of that. I'd flipped through Marcin's prints as he shared his ideas.

An underground casino on the Southside. An illegal strip club owned by Hasidim. Then there was the waterfront—if you went there for five minutes, you knew it was a story, and I was hot to be a journalist.

Marcin's photos were compelling—a wedding at the Russian Orthodox Church on North Eleventh with the cleric wearing more bling than Jay-Z, an explosion of pigeons at McCarren Park, a pretty young Latina waiting alone at a bus kiosk on North Seventh. No one in the photos noticed Marcin; invisibility was the special quality he brought to his art. I didn't trust him—how could you?—but he had energy and he could see.

We left the basement and walked west through a shabby corridor of row houses. Polish grandmothers in housedresses swept their walks or leaned on padded elbows at their windows. The block before the water the houses gave way to warehouses in varying states of decay. An Italian bar/restaurant, Io, had just opened in a renovated brick building on Kent across from the waste transfer station between North Fifth and Seventh. I'd gone to the bar a couple of times to watch pirated pay-per-view fights. Rumor had it that the restaurant was Mob-owned (rumor said the same thing about Baretti Carting Corporation, which owned the transfer station). A high fence surrounded the lot between North Seventh and Ninth but there was always a hole and we pushed through onto a loading dock.

Late September had gentled the summer—no more crushing sun and clotted air. A breeze bowed the cattails. Across the river Manhattan gleamed. From the rustic fields the towers looked like a hallucination. A seaplane blustered onto the river from some mooring and then rose and arced over our heads. The usual Williamsburg mélange had decamped to the water. Polish women—fat ladies in one-pieces and their daughters in bikinis, sullen and stacked—sunbathed on the loading docks. Latinos with Styrofoam coolers and transistor radios fished off the piers. Couples sat on the long bulkhead wall and dog walkers let their animals roam. From the end of a loading dock came the bleats and blats of musicians at work, horns and bass drum and calls to time. The ragtag players wore the shakos and piped jackets of a high school marching band, mismatched with miniskirts and denim.

Mild weather and open space made everyone amicable, all nods and smiles. The Dominican teenagers didn't side-arm rocks at the freaks in the band. The art-school refugees didn't giggle at the homeless. Even the Polish bathing beauties said hello. We'd dropped our city masks for the day. As Marcin and I came to the bulkhead I noticed a man walking into the water from the riprap shore between the bulkhead and the first pier. He was lean, smoothly muscled and no older than thirty, and he was wearing a red Speedo. I'd seen him before—you didn't forget a red Speedo, not on that waterfront of broken glass. When he got knee-deep he pulled up his goggles, dove and began to swim, a slow crawl out to the end of the pier and back and then out again.

A young black woman watched him from the shore. She wore a ragged sweater and had a short Afro.

Hi there, she said as we walked by.

Hello, I said.

My name is Brandi, she said, and stretched her hands toward the sun. Loose sleeves slid down scabbed arms.

Look at him, she said. Isn't he handsome?

Definitely, I said, watching the steady strokes out to the pier edge and back.

She leaned closer. Her sweet smile lacked two front teeth.

I'm going to have his baby, she said.

Congratulations, I said.

He's never touched me sexually, she said, but it would be a beautiful child. He has green eyes. He protects me. This place can be dangerous. One time we found a cut-off arm in the weeds.

There on the shoreline she started to dance. Marcin took photos. Directly behind us was a big Dumpster, one side torn free. Inside were a cot and an armchair—on the Upper East Side you could have rented it for $850 a month. Brandi pirouetted and then her shuffling dance stopped. She hugged herself and rubbed her arms. She looked at me sidelong under her lashes, a little sly.

I'm very fond of the brownies they have at the bakery up the street, she said. Do you think you can give me a dollar?

I found a dollar in my pocket and we walked away from her out to the pier. We watched the swimmer rise from the water and wade to Brandi on the shore.

I see her sometimes, Marcin said. She stands on the corner near Kokie's. Where there are all the trucks.

Marcin meant that she was one of the prostitutes who worked the side streets around Kent.

Why don't you write about her? Marcin said.

Most living things, from lowly bacteria to Homo saps, easily convert glucose molecules to energy. In hot, dry factory air, the potential energy stored in sugar inclined toward combustion. Conflagration marked New York sugar history— January 8, 1882, Havemeyer and Elder plant in Williamsburg, destroyed; another Havemeyer plant, in Greenpoint in 1887, blam!; the Dick and Meyer sugar refinery in Williamsburg, September 7, 1889, a Roman candle on the river. Even the refineries that survived couldn't keep up with replacing windows that the explosions burst. In old photos you see shattered window frames, a premonition of future dereliction. At the refineries the filters and kilns, centrifuges and vacuum pans, needed to be fed, and coal and water poured into steam engines. To bring sugar to alabaster perfection required one final step, a secret ingredient. That ingredient was bone char, also called 'ivory black.' Fortunately, the extermination of the buffalo had littered the plains with the perfect raw material. Railroad cars loaded with buffalo skeletons clanked into the Eastern District Station on North Fifth to make sugar pure.

To Harry Havemeyer the Williamsburg waterfront in 1987 was as dead as *Bison bison*. Between South Second and South Fifth Streets the last of the 'Rhenish castles,' the Havemeyer and Elder plant built by Harry's grandfather, still operated—as Domino Sugar—at a fraction of capacity (over 950 million tons a year). Domino had moved production to Louisiana, to Mexico and Brazil, places where the sun blazed and unions were weak.

Directly north of the diminished refinery, sentry boxes and barbed wire guarded the storage tanks of the New England Petroleum Company. Beyond them stood the white block of the Austin, Nichols & Company Warehouse, built by Havemeyer and Elder in 1915. It 'appears to be in use,' Harry wrote after seeing lights in the upper floors. Those lights had been brought by artists living there illegally.

Once a terminal for the Pennsylvania Railroad, the block between North Fourth and North Fifth Streets was 'a scrap metal yard filled with crushed cars and other junk.' Farther north on the waterfront Harry found more of the same. 'The Havemeyer & Elder-Brooklyn Eastern District Terminal property north of North Fifth Street is completely silent. Its few warehouses and office buildings are abandoned, broken and burned-out husks. As a result of railroad bankruptcy, nothing of value is left at all. That waterfront land, the "priceless gem" of past times, is now owned by the City of New York, which took it over in lieu of unpaid taxes.'

Broken windows and marsh grass, bushes and tree roots rupturing loading docks, crumbling piers. Industrial Williamsburg was dead and gone.

'It is available,' Havemeyer wrote, 'to any interested buyer.'

On the Waterfront

Harry Havemeyer was right about the waterfront: it was a gem. I had no particular justification for going there—it didn't make me smarter or richer, didn't give me a line on my CV or increase my chances of getting laid. My waterfront ran from the Bayside Fuel Oil tanks on North Twelfth all the way south to Domino Sugar. By year two in the neighborhood I had learned to navigate that corridor. You needed denim and long sleeves because you crawled under fences, vaulted razor wire and pushed through thorns—the shoreline had become second-growth forest. You climbed walls and edged out along broken docks that made a rusty trapeze. On most of the trail the loudest sound was wave-slap against shore, the only witness the gleaming metal face of Manhattan. What you saw made the thorn punctures and wire cuts worthwhile—seabirds, the broken factories of the old order, sweet views of skyscrapers. On the Fourth of July, I'd navigate the fences and trees to a rocky breakwater where I'd sit and watch the fireworks, my private show, so alone, so far from the cops and crowds on Kent Avenue that I felt rich.

To all the Brooklyn folks surprised to learn that you live on Long Island (I know you're out there), please consult a map: New York City is surrounded by water, four of the five boroughs on three islands. Water made the city, from its Dutch trading post days through the 1940s when it was the largest port in the world. As the Commissioners of Streets and Roads noted in 1807 by way of excusing the lack of parkland in their city plan: 'those large arms of the sea which embrace Manhattan Island, render its situation, in regard to health and pleasure, as well as to convenience and commerce, peculiarly felicitous.' Translation: who needs parks when you have an ocean?

A strange thing happened in the decades after World War II: New York turned its back on the water. No more ocean liner fleet at the West Side piers, no more freighters nestled up to Brooklyn docks, no more destroyers launching from the navy yard below Vinegar Hill. It became almost impossible to make your way to the shore. Expressways ringed it, cutting off the approaches like an asphalt moat stocked with mechanical crocodiles. Even in the places where you could get through, the water was fifteen feet down the side of a pier and opaque with filth. Joe Mitchell's 1950s *New Yorker* pieces about paddling around the harbor talking to fishermen read like science fiction (my literary agency represented his estate and I'd swiped his complete works from the office). By 1995 the Brooklyn waterfront was a toxic wasteland from Newton Creek and its oil spill to the ruined docks of Red Hook. The capital of the twentieth century stood knee-deep in a sewer. Yet the rot provided opportunity. There were holes in the fences. Mitchell had been stopped and grilled at the waterfront by cops infected with Cold War paranoia; we could reach the water without a second look.

The waterfront I navigated in jeans and boots was the waterfront for the daredevil, the urban Indiana Jones. It also contained a more sedentary stretch. Between Bayside Fuel and a 'waste transfer station' on North Sixth the waterfront opened. Those five blocks contained three defunct factories, four abandoned warehouses, two concrete loading docks and three piers topped by meadow and forest. In the open spaces nature had returned, all high grass and bushes and marsh. You went there for the breezes and the open space and for the views. The views were as good as the one from the Brooklyn Heights Promenade except that on the Northside the freeway didn't shake the ground and you could walk all the way to the river.

Beside one of the loading docks an antique fire hydrant leaked into an iron bathtub. Overflow from the tub fed a marshy pool bordered with long grass and cattails. Dragonflies hovered over the pool and flocks of small birds seamed the grass. You could hear wavelets break and gulls croak and traffic hum on the FDR Drive all the way across the East River. I'd walk to the end of the longest pier and step off the edge onto a narrow mooring that led to a piling. The guanoed posts shifted and rocked as I sat looking at tugs and seaplanes. Circle Line tour boats churned by and tourists waved. I waved back.

When I was nine or ten my friends and I made a trail that ran through backyards down our entire block. Parents couldn't see us there. It was better than the world of school and television; there were newts and millipedes, slopes covered with pine needles and trees to climb. One section of the trail ran across a retaining wall behind a garage. The retaining wall rose fifteen feet above the yard below. A magnolia filled the yard and every spring it turned into a chandelier.

I'd sit there and stare at the soundless explosion in purple and white. I didn't know anything about trees or flowers but the magnolia held me.

The fact that the Williamsburg waterfront stayed open, well, that was a historical accident. Our playground had come within a couple of borough council votes of being a Wal-Mart or a garbage dump. The Manhattan skyline made you appreciate the waterfront even more: you were in a quiet place away from crowds and noise and struggle. Of course the waterfront belonged to somebody—somebody biding his time—and that somebody had put a fence around it. There were plenty of ways around the fence but we cut holes in it to make a point. And when the fences were repaired, we cut new holes. You never saw a cop down there. It wasn't necessarily safe. If I went at night I'd carry a heavy stick.

All kinds of wannabes and freaks and romantics who'd been priced out of the East Village went to the waterfront. Impromptu sculptures made of paving stones rose over my head. I remember the word-of-mouth outdoor screenings, films projected against the back wall of a warehouse. One of the factories had a sculpture garden in front of it with welded metal and massive broken columns. The sculptor was a black cowboy—ten-gallon hat, boots and all. He told me that he lived in the factory and that the owner tolerated him because he deterred looters. An old truck sheltered under a tin awning next to the factory. The truck was at least thirty years old; you could tell by the antiquated grille. It looked like it had been parked there on the last day of work and forgotten. Brush grew over the cab windows.

I brought dates to the waterfront because there wasn't a better place to drink a bottle of wine. It was a test for the women; they had to trust that this stranger wasn't a psychopath. All of them said yes. Over the years, I broke into all the abandoned buildings. In one I found gigantic metal cylinders and chutes. The stairwell of another was so jammed with desks and chairs that you could only get through by climbing over them. In another building neatly made cots lined the clean-swept second floor. It looked like a dormitory—a dormitory with broken windows and million-dollar views. For me the waterfront was the hinterland of the only neighborhood that I'd ever thought of as mine. Exploration turned me into an amateur archaeologist. I wondered what the metal cylinders were for—grain, cement, oil? I tried to understand the impulse that led to the chairs and desks cramming the stairwell—they must have been piled up to keep people out. I considered the cots, sitting there like a peasant camp on the floor of the Colosseum in the eighth century A.D.

The waterfront belonged to me, and to no one—which meant it was used for more than sun worship and band practice. Garbage got dumped in the thick brush, the mounds rising forty bags high. Some drivers from the waste transfer station on the next lot lightened their loads in the open space. Cars ended up there too, dumped and burned, the frames twisted by fire. The charred shells marked the end of joyrides, or so the arsonists wanted their insurance companies to think.

People lived on the waterfront: the 'deinstitutionalized' insane, those prostitutes—and their pimps—who worked the truck stop near Kokie's, migrant Mexicans who broke down old freight containers by hand and sold the aluminum scrap. An Albanian refugee built an elaborate wooden shanty on the edge of a loading dock and painted 'Fuck the Serbs' on one plywood wall. Homeless men lived in the buildings or in tents or Dumpsters or shanties made of plywood and debris. They bathed at the iron tub next to the hydrant. Shampoo bottles and soap slivers speckled the ground and soap scum rimed one shore of the pool. On the waterfront all these different groups shaded into one another: I knew art-school kids who crashed there because they were new to town and broke or losing their minds.

Sometimes you couldn't tell if the odd formations were the work of man or chance. In the warehouses and on a loading dock, I started noticing arrangements of old tin cans, broken dolls, Polaroid snapshots and random auto parts. It wasn't Joseph Cornell but the impulse was the same. One day I walked into a warehouse to find a Latino with a white cloud of hair arranging trash on the floor, then leaning back to contemplate his handiwork. I'd seen him pushing a bicycle around the neighborhood, sacks filled with bottles and cans tied to handlebars and frame. When he noticed me, he hurried away with his bike and bags and I walked to where he'd been messing around. When I saw the trash I realized that the old man was an artist. To highlight his creation, he'd swept the floor around the offerings.

Chris II

So let's hang out, one of Chris's friends would say.

Sounds good, Chris would say. Where?

Your neighborhood. Williamsburg. Greenpoint. I'll drive over.

Uhhhh . . . okay, Chris would say. But you do know that there's nothing to do here. You know that, right?

It's cool, the friend would say.

Going into Queens College, Chris knew that he wanted to be a writer. He didn't know what that meant exactly but it gave him a direction and at Queens there were a few other students who read books, and adults who appreciated students who read books. The pop culture zeitgeist had caught up to Chris: grunge, with its metal edge and punk bravado, was the sound he had been waiting for. Chris also had the coolest job any eighteen-year-old could hope for—bike messenger.

I'm riding around in between classes, Chris says, kneeing cabs and shit. I was like Eddie Vedder in combat boots with hair down my back. In rain pouring down, with a messenger bag on my back. I loved it.

But Chris still lived in the great nowhere.

So when his friends came over and there was nothing to do, they did what teenagers do when there's nothing to do: they roamed. One thing Williamsburg gave them was plenty of space for roaming.

What you would end up doing, Chris says, is just breaking into stuff and exploring it. That's what I kind of did. And it was pitch-black. Half the lights weren't really working. Even the waterfront, which was gorgeous, was a shoreline of busted glass. Shining with busted glass everywhere.

They climbed into buildings, skimmed rocks on the river, poked around in the brush. ('We were like the guys in *Stand by Me*,' Chris says. 'Without the woods.') They broke into the immense industrial castle of the pencil factory on Franklin Street and played manhunt across the roofs until cops and security guards got into the game. They broke into McCarren Park Pool, because that's something you had to do if you were a neighborhood kid. A ship had been scuttled off the North Tenth pier and they hopped onto the half-sunken deck. (A few years later, Chris and one of his first girlfriends would have sex there, frequently, her shoulders pressed to the cold steel wall.)

For outsiders, Chris had a special destination: the Semer Sleep Mattress factory over the rock-strewn soccer field on the east side of McCarren Park.

The original frame of that building was six stories, Chris says. Before they built whatever the fuck that is on top of it now [he means condos]. You could easily bust in there by going underneath a fence and climbing up a rickety stairwell in the back. And then we'd climb up to the water towers that were on the top and sit there and the view was just stunning. We had a million-dollar view of the city and nobody gave a fuck. Because nobody else wanted it, it belonged to us.

Cold weather changed the waterfront. The cattails turned yellow. Strong winds blew off the river, and the tarps on the shanties flapped. The sunbathers went away. It was just Marcin and me, Marcin stopping to shoot as I shivered and hopped. On our winter scouting mission we saw a woman crawl out of a hole in a warehouse wall and pull a knit cap down over her ears.

That's her, Marcin said.

Her? I moved closer. It was Brandi.

Go talk to her, Marcin said.

It felt awkward. I wasn't much of a journalist. I wondered what I would say: 'Hey Brandi, remember me? I gave you a dollar for a brownie. So, what's it like turning tricks for truckers and Hasids?' Recently, two prostitutes had been murdered near the waterfront. The story was that the Mafia owners of Io hadn't appreciated whores on parade across from their respectable business. The restaurant was reputed to have been financed by a loan from the Bank of Credit and Commerce International. BCCI had funded model citizens like the mujahideen and the contras (Ollie North had several BCCI accounts). The money the prostitutes used to buy crack sold by the Mafia was laundered by BCCI, which gave loans to the mobsters who hired the hit men to kill the prostitutes. In effect, the prostitutes were paying BCCI for their deaths. I wanted to find out more but had no idea how.

Hi, I said after I walked up to her.

She looked at me, her eyes clouded and red.

We met before, I said. Your friend was swimming in the river.

Brandi harrumphed. She scratched. The wind threw icicles at us that never missed. I didn't know how to ask about dead women or her accommodations or a job description.

I gotta go, she said. She pulled her cap down tight and set off across the field toward the truck stop. Marcin looked at me with disapproval. He was taking pictures, what was I doing?

Since the summer, Brandi's building had been fortified with a circle of brush and razor wire. The hole was some eight feet up the wall at the top of a dirt mound. It looked like a direct hit from a mortar shell.

Let's go, Marcin said. I was amenable.

We climbed the rubble to the breach. Pushing our heads through to darkness, we heard guttural barking and something heavy rushed toward us. As we slid back down the mound, a large animal jumped through the hole. Light framed a pit bull, thick and menacing. It scrambled toward us, barking. The photographer and the writer ran across the frozen ground, pit bull at their heels.

Ethical Heroin

The teenage boy sat up in his narrow bed. While Marcin and I looked on, the boy fished a small packet from the top of his nightstand, pried it open and dumped white powder onto a hand mirror. Then he took a short straw from the nightstand and inserted it into a nostril. It was around noon on a Tuesday.

I don't want to lose any heroin on the sides, Sham said, gesturing at his nose. I want it to go straight to my brain.

When I'd met Sham the previous Saturday, he told me that he was kicking on Monday. But on Monday night he did a speedball and got drunk with 'some Chicago guys.'

With a half inch of straw protruding from his nose, he leaned over the powder and inhaled deeply. He pulled out the straw, pinched the opposite nostril and snorted again. He threw back his head. Sham was ready to start his day.

The most promising story idea that Marcin brought to me was about teenage Polish heroin addicts. He said that the neighborhood was full of them. He showed me photos of kids like Sham shooting up, including a girl who looked to be about twelve. The photos were dramatic—deep shadow and soft light, arms tied off, intense expressions of children gathered around the needle. I shopped the story to *The Village Voice* and they were interested. Sham was my first interview.

Those Chicago guys are into some bad stuff, he said. I know, because one day they have no money, and the next day they have a lot.

I soon figured out that 'bad stuff' meant stealing cars and selling drugs.

Look at that, he said, pointing to a poster on the

wall. That's from a party I DJ'd a few weeks ago. My real name is . . .

He said something gutturally Polish along the lines of 'Prezeminik.'

. . . but you can call me Sham. That's my DJ name. DJ Shamrock.

Sure enough, 'DJ Shamrock' appeared near the bottom of a poster smeared in Day-Glo colors. Other music posters filled the walls and there was a double DJ turntable on a desk covered in CDs and cassettes. Sham was fifteen and I didn't think it had been long since the walls of his room had held posters of Conan and Michael Jordan.

My turntables are busted, he said. And I can't afford new ones. Usually I spin jungle, techno and hardcore grooves. Then I do some mixing and scratching on my tables. Or at least I used to.

He told us that he had designed the poster on his computer illustrator program but, like the turntables, the computer was broken.

I can't even turn the thing on, he said.

Sham put on a jungle mix, then moved on to his second bag of dope. Just the first bag would have been enough to make me vomit for six hours, but for Sham it was coffee. He pulled out the straw, inhaled one last time and wiped his nose with a forearm.

Those artists who live around here, he said, they do a lot of dope, right?

I'm not sure, I said. Some of them. People lie about it.

What kind of music do they listen to?

As I stammered out an answer, Sham led us into the main room of the apartment. It had a stove and a bathtub three feet apart, and a foldout couch where his mother slept.

On a table next to the couch, Mom had left a stack of waffles. A bottle of maple syrup stood next to the stack. Half a dozen sausage links hung from the shower curtain rod, cloth napkins between sausage and rod. Sham noticed my glance.

Kielbasa, he said. You let it hang there for a few days and then you cook it in the microwave.

He smacked his lips.

It tastes fantastic, he said.

The house was on North Fifth and like mine it lay at the back of a narrow lot. Instead of another building screening it, the lot had a yard with a garden and laundry lines. Sham's mother was at her office job. It was a school day but Sham didn't seem particularly worried about playing hooky.

I want to get a car, he said. You need a car in New York City.

He smirked.

Of course, he said, to get a car you need a job.

I liked Sham's energy and sense of humor. So far drugs hadn't degraded him. He was pale and thin but muscle swelled under his singlet and he was handsome in a Polish way, with high cheekbones and light blue eyes. He poured maple syrup onto a waffle, folded it and ate it in two bites. He said he wanted to get a job. He said he wanted to get his own apartment. In the summer, the Chicago guys were going to take him to the Second City.

They have a Polish neighborhood like Greenpoint, he said. Except stupider.

A few weeks earlier, I'd started seeing a very young, very pretty blonde leaving Marcin's apartment. It didn't take long for Marcin to tell me about her—Magda was a model and fifteen (or fourteen, Marcin didn't keep his story straight).

He showed me nude photos of her. She lay on his couch, head tipped back over the armless edge so that her small breasts jutted up from her chest. Every rib showed. For the most part she looked like what she was: a skinny kid. But her eyes were enormous and a color I'd never seen before, a deep, creamy blue. I realized one reason her eyes were so striking was that her pupils were so small, and her pupils were so small because she was high.

Magda and I ran into each other in the courtyard when Marcin was at work. She told me how much she hated modeling—the long waits in offices, the bickering and competition among the girls. 'It's tough,' she said. 'You don't make money in New York.'

When Magda wasn't modeled up in heels and tight skirts she wore a punk uniform of black jeans, T-shirt and smudged black eyeliner. One day when she locked herself out of Marcin's apartment she invited herself into mine. She crawled through my second-story window and dropped into the backyard so that she could break into his place. Not too many models would have done that.

Two nights after my first 'interview' with Sham I went to Greenpoint with him so I could see him score. Sham's plan was to buy heroin from a dealer who hung out at the park side of Manhattan Avenue. We walked from Norman to Driggs and stopped beside a dark warehouse. No dealer. The commercial strip of Manhattan Avenue ended there. Further east were empty factories and the ruin of McCarren Park Pool.

Give me a cigarette, Sham said.

Sorry, I said. I don't smoke.

I come here every morning before school, Sham said. All

my friends meet on this block. Sometimes we go to the courts. If there's nothing to do, we just go to school.

We turned down Driggs and crossed into McCarren Park, the fields dark and quiet. A few late-night dog walkers milled around center field, their animals whirling shadows.

Usually my friends chill here, he said. But the cops have been chasing them off.

As we walked, Sham scooped coke from a plastic baggie with his little finger and shoved it up his nose. He hadn't forgotten about kicking.

I'm a little worried about it, he said. My friend quit and by the next day he was hallucinating. He was so fucked up he left his car in the middle of the street with the door open and the keys in the ignition. He passed out on my couch and when he woke up he started shouting, 'Where's my car?' We spent an hour looking for it. Another friend of mine got out of rehab and the next day he was shooting up again. Did you ever shoot up?

I said that I hadn't.

Me neither, Sham said. I'm definitely going to try it, though.

I didn't mention that I'd seen him in Marcin's photos with a needle in his arm.

Sham led us out of the park onto Bedford. A car booming techno sped by and honked. Sham waved.

That's some of the Chicago guys, he said. Maybe they can hook us up.

He ran down the street, legs kicking high, trying to catch them at the light on Nassau.

You know, Robert, Marcin said.

We were down in the basement, where the sun was a

stranger. I loved the way Marcin pronounced my name, rolling the *r*'s and stressing the last syllable so that he always sounded happy to see me.

You know, he said, I was the first person to give Prezamik heroin. (Marcin always used Sham's Polish name.)

I was shooting the Pulaski Day Parade in Greenpoint, he said, when I noticed a group of Polish skater boys coming out of the subway. I started to shoot and they came over. I told them I wanted to shoot them skating and Prezamik was the most interested.

I wanted to see the boys rising from the subway with Marcin's eyes. They were trying to swagger but their rubber legs and light frames bounced, boards jammed under their arms, the sullen set to their faces cracking at the spectacle of the parade.

Now, Marcin said, more than half of them are heroin addicts.

Marcin told me that he had run into Sham on the street one day and that Sham had offered to get his cool new friend drugs—pot, coke, crack. 'I don't use any of that shit,' Marcin said. 'But you're high,' the ever-observant Sham replied. Marcin reached into his pocket and pulled out a bag. 'This is what I use,' he said, and gave Sham a taste.

After that, Sham called Marcin every day, wanting to score. After a few weeks, Marcin took the boy to his favorite corner, South First and Hooper, and made the introductions. Sham in turn became the source for the Polish skate punks of Greenpoint. Then he made a rookie mistake—he brought a friend with him to the corner and broke his own monopoly. Losing his customers stranded Sham with a four-bag-a-day heroin habit: $280 a week, a tough nut for a working-class kid who didn't have a job.

I watched Marcin absently scratch one leg in junkie

default motion. Since we'd started the article, I'd been spending more time in his cave. The rooms held all the paraphernalia of the aspiring artist—piles of novels and art books, odd artifacts like an old-fashioned iron (no electricity necessary; you heated it on the range top), art posters and framed prints of Marcin's photos on the walls. On the floor you could see where the old floorboards gave way to new planks Marcin had added. Important phone numbers were written on the yellow walls in pink Sharpie.

How many of those kids are addicted? I said.

I don't know, Marcin said. Maybe fifty.

And they all started getting heroin from you?

Marcin smiled.

Robert, he said. Didn't you know? I am the divvel.

Some of the kids had jumped straight from cigarettes to dope: no gateway drugs for them.

Marcin had come to the U.S. as a teenager with his mother, a quiet, sickly woman who worked in a Manhattan Avenue bank. After a year in Greenpoint, Marcin had found a share with some local artist kids, including Justin, who had grown up in a basement apartment on Berry. The windows opened to a sewer grate. Justin had gotten Marcin a job at a photo studio, which paid well enough to cover Marcin's rent and keep him in heroin. A Puerto Rican coworker had brought him to the prime corner.

I was using six bags a day, Marcin said. But I'm much better now. I'm kicking slowly. I still have a problem. But it's not so bad.

Marcin showed me other photos of Magda—naked except for the rubber tube tying off her arm. Marcin had introduced Magda to heroin also, and she'd gone on to supply other models at her agency on West Broadway. The heroin octopus had stretched his tentacles from a corner on the Southside to Greenpoint, through Marcin's apartment and across the river to plush Manhattan lobbies where Magda and the other teenage girls waited with their portfolios.

I looked at him, his hands trembling, his rough-cut hair dyed black, the stubble on his cheeks so intermittent you could measure the space between hairs in centimeters. Marcin was a carrier, a disease vector, his thin, pale figure in black jeans bearing heroin between the various cultures of Williamsburg—Poles, artists, Latinos, junkies. The Southside had been a heroin depot since the 1960s and there were plenty of other drugs floating around Greenpoint too (although not much dope). But it took someone like Marcin, young, rootless, curious, amoral, to connect Polish Greenpoint skate kids to sketchy dealers wearing shades and lounging around Borinquen Place, and from there to connect models in SoHo to the Southside.

Yet Marcin was only the most louche harbinger of change. Artists were warping the fabric of the neighborhood with their energies and their tastes. Most of them wanted peace, time to work and a place to call home, more Roger Williams than William Bradford. For the natives the character of the colonizer didn't matter; they got diphtheria either way. Change was burning through Williamsburg. If you lacked antibodies you'd be pushed out or extinguished; if you had defenses, then you could transform opportunity into gold, which was why immigrants had come to shithole Williamsburg from much deeper shitholes in Santo Domingo and Warsaw.

·

We need money! a voice said on the speakerphone.

We need money, the voice repeated.

Other voices rose in the background, a distorted bellow. So we can get dope!

I was in the basement a couple of weeks after Marcin revealed himself as the 'divvel.' Magda had dumped him, which seemed to bother Marcin not at all. Magda's replacement sat with us, listening to Sham holler for drugs. She'd met Marcin in a photography class at the School of Visual Arts. Judith had dark, solemn eyes, plush lips and glossy skin. I'd met her in the courtyard the morning after their punk rock honeymoon, both of them sleepless and reeking of pot and sex, pupils so swollen I assumed they were tripping. Judith moved in days later and she sat on the couch where Magda had stretched for the camera.

You still there, Marcin? Sham said.

I have to go, Marcin said. I call you later.

He hung up and smiled at me.

I had no idea why Sham thought Marcin owed him money and the photographer didn't enlighten me.

They are having a party tonight, Marcin said. So they want drugs.

I'd talked to the corrections officer for the Greenpoint police precinct. In a brusque Queens accent she told me that, no, she hadn't noticed any increase in drug abuse among Polish teenagers, and just who was I writing for anyway? That same afternoon, I ran into Sham at a Bedford bodega. In natural light he looked tired and even younger. He asked me for money for his help with the article. When I told him I couldn't pay him to talk to me, he'd walked out of the store. The entire project was floating beyond my reach.

·

I have to talk to you, Magda said.

Magda had walked into the L Café with a friend as I sat at my usual station. The friend was another Polish girl, in a long pleated skirt, a little plump, a little dowdy, with zits on her forehead. A normal fifteen-year-old girl. The girls took a table, then Magda came over and knelt beside me, looking up.

It's about those photos Marcin showed you, she said.

A tight blouse hugged her slender chest. The blouse had horizontal blue and white stripes and matched her blue-and-white knee socks. Ivory thighs emerged from her dark blue skirt. She looked nothing at all like a fifteen-year-old girl.

You know that Marcin is the one who gave me dope for the first time, right? she said. And he taught us all to shoot.

He told me, I said.

He took me with him to score, she said. So I tried it. But I'm not in that place anymore.

I assumed she was telling me that she'd stopped using. It was a very different story from the one she'd given me a few weeks earlier, when she said that she had never used and that Marcin no longer did.

I'm not all the way back, though, she said.

Her teeth were crooked, one canine jutting forward. That couldn't have helped in her business. But she had perfect skin and full red lips. And those eyes, those big eyes cobalt and cream. Her pupils were dots, specks, flecks. It didn't seem that they let in enough light for her to see.

I'm not high, she said, suddenly telepathic. My pupils just do that on their own. They're always small.

I didn't believe her.

So those photos that Marcin took? The ones with us all shooting up?

Yeah, I said, he showed me those.

The Voice loved Marcin's photos.

Well, she said. That other girl in the photos. The one with Sham? She would never use. She was just attracted to Marcin, so . . .

She shrugged.

And Sham, she said, would never use needles.

I'm sure, I said.

I hate this, Magda said. It's like with my last agency. They were always saying, 'This client is so hot for you.' But then they never paid me. I'm with another agency now.

She gave me a hug and said goodbye. I embraced a skeleton with a baby-fat face. Sometimes Magda looked like a child and other times she looked like a *Marie Claire* moon goddess. Other times she looked like . . . like an old woman. There was an air of age around her, like her life had been accelerated.

The article was dead. I didn't have any facts that I could trust, and even if I did, not even *The Voice* was going to run a piece about how their photographer scored dope for his subjects.

In the following weeks I'd see Marcin and Judith in the yard or hear them through windows that had opened with warm weather. They were busy out there, planting flowers and herbs with spring, uprooting bushes and weeds that had sprouted through the concrete. They chattered and puttered around in old clothes: simple country life at the cottage. One afternoon I heard more banging and looked out to see Marcin shattering concrete with a nine-pound sledgehammer, opening space for a garden. He was making the city bloom. I went out to see if I could take a couple of swings.

Marcin went cold turkey, Judith said. He hasn't done dope for two weeks.

She beamed at her working man. I didn't tell her that I'd seen Marcin the day before and he'd called Sham in search of dope. When Judith went inside, I gave him the latest news.

I saw Magda in the L, I said. She told me that those photos of the kids shooting up were all staged. That they weren't really using.

Marcin smiled his wry smile.

Robert, he said, you have to realize that we are dealing with junkies here. You have to be careful. You can't trust anything they say.

A few days later I ran into Sham on Bedford. His wifebeater and jeans were encrusted with dirt. The filth came from a good cause.

I worked today, he said.

That's great, I said.

My cousin got me the job, he said. It was for this builder in Bushwick. Five fifty an hour. Demolition and drywall.

I've done that kind of stuff too, I said.

Magda's been calling me, he said. She wants me to score a bindle for her. I think she needs it because she's going to England.

So did you hook her up?

I'm quitting, he said. I'm getting two bottles of methadone tonight. From a friend of mine. I'm trading my new skateboard for it.

I knew that he'd gotten the skateboard from Marcin but I didn't mention it. I was tired of keeping up with their transactions: if Marcin gave Sham the skateboard to cover a debt, if it was a loan, if there really is methadone at the end of the rainbow.

Good luck, man, I said, and shook his hand.

In the yard, Marcin held a paintbrush and laid white strokes on a long wooden table. He was shirtless and thin and I admired the abstract tattoos that wrapped his upper arms. I told him Sham's methadone story but he had a story to top it.

I went to Beth Israel last week, he said. To enroll in the methadone program they have. If you're below a certain income level it only costs thirty dollars a week.

He drew smooth lines with the brush, focused on the whitewashing.

But the doctor there told me to kick cold turkey. He said that most addicts end up using both the methadone and heroin at the same time.

Marcin looked up from the table.

The doctor said, 'You look like a smart guy. So if you really want to quit, that's the way to do it.' It's not fun. You are sick. Very sick. For four or five days. You sweat. You shit. You shiver. The important thing is to stay in the bathtub.

A friend of mine is coming over to help me, Marcin said. In two weeks I'm going to Chicago to visit Judith's family. I want to be clean before I get there.

He wiped his forehead with the hand holding the brush. White droplets fell to the concrete. I could only imagine what a Jewish suburban doctor would make of the black-eyed Gypsy (but then, I'd been the Gypsy at Rebecca's holiday dinners in Rockland County).

There's a big Polish community there, he said. I want to shoot it. You know, what's going on.

Maybe you should go to some NA meetings, I said.

I gave him the number of a college friend of mine who'd gone down a similar road. In her junkie days she'd helped a boyfriend rob people at ATMs and finally gotten arrested. 'How can a girl like you, who went to Sarah Lawrence College, stoop to such behavior?' the judge had intoned. But he let her off with rehab. When I had coffee with her at the L, she told me she was working for CBS.

You know, I saw Sham yesterday on the street, Marcin said. He started yelling at me, threatening to kill me.

For what?

For showing you those needle photos, Marcin said. In the middle of Bedford he was yelling, 'I'll kill you myself. I won't even use another guy.' He was really upset.

Marcin seemed surprised.

So what are you going to do? I said.

It was nothing, Marcin said. We went to the store and I bought him an ice cream. You know, to raise his blood sugar.

I'm really not addicted, Marcin said.

It was a hot day, the first heat wave of early summer, sidewalk throwing sharp light into my face, sun bludgeoning the back of my head. Marcin was leaving for Chicago the next day and he'd offered to take me to the heroin depot before he left. I'd abandoned all hope for the article but I was still curious. So much had been said about the place, so much trouble had come from it.

We walked east toward Bushwick.

When I stop, Marcin said, it's not that big a deal. I don't get sick. I still go to work. I had to do this shoot at MoMA once when I was really strung out. I was shaky and sweating, and I got so dizzy. But I finished the job.

On the other side of the BQE we passed a pool supply store. The words 'thriving business' didn't come to mind when I saw the missing letters on the sign. Not many people in Williamsburg were buying pools. Then came Kellogg's Diner, favorite late-night haunt of cops, city workers and the gloriously inebriated. Marcin mentioned a local car service office.

I once bought twenty bags there, Marcin said. So they brought me into the back. They had a really nice scale. I felt like I was in a movie.

I'd waited there one night with a friend of Rebecca's until a car showed up. I believe she was wearing a fur.

One of the skater kids got murdered last week, Marcin said. An older junkie did it. Slit his throat. They haven't found the body but everybody knows what happened.

I didn't answer. It could have been a real tragedy or more junkie talk, I couldn't tell the difference. Of course there was no body; a body would have meant facts. A body would have meant an article. There were facts and then there were facts, and I didn't have the right kind. Marcin said one thing. Magda said something else. Sham didn't agree. I couldn't be everywhere at once and even that wouldn't be enough. I needed a certain kind of fact to translate their stories into journalism, but the essence of the stories didn't rest in things I could verify. Dates and names and places didn't seem to reach what was happening. The story was in the contradictions, in impressions that curled in the air and faded away. I wasn't a good enough journalist to make an article out of that.

We turned the corner at Grand and walked to South First and Hooper: and there was the spot. My first Williamsburg apartment, the share with Rose, was only a block and a half away. Marcin had finally provided an explanation for the drug zombies I'd always had to dodge at my doorstep. Scaffolding wrapped the tenement building and a few Hispanic men took cover in the shade, not talking to each other, just waiting. I went back up the block and stood across the street from the Apolo Restaurant. When Rose was feeling too lazy to walk the dog, which was often, she would lead him up to the roof to shit. Tattered curtains flounced in the windows. I wondered if she still lived there.

I'm not buying for myself, Marcin said when he reappeared. But please don't say anything to Judith.

3

Mad White People

1997–1999

There are two elements, at least, that are essential to Bohemianism. The first is devotion or addiction to one or more of the Seven Arts; the other is poverty . . . I like to think of my Bohemians as young, as radical in their outlook on art and life; as unconventional, and . . . as dwellers in a city large enough to have the somewhat cruel atmosphere of all great cities.　　—George Sterling, in a letter to Jack London

To take the world as one finds it, the bad with the good, making the best of the present moment—to laugh at Fortune alike whether she be generous or unkind—to spend freely when one has money, and to hope gaily when one has none—to fleet the time carelessly, living for love and art—this is the temper and spirit of the modern Bohemian . . . In Bohemia one may find almost every sin save that of Hypocrisy. [The Bohemian's] faults are more commonly those of self-indulgence, thoughtlessness, vanity and procrastination, and these usually go hand-in-hand with generosity, love and charity; for it is not enough to be one's self in Bohemia, one must allow others to be themselves, as well. What, then, is it that makes this mystical empire of Bohemia unique, and what is the charm of its mental fairyland? It is this: there are no roads in all Bohemia! One must choose and find one's own path, be one's own self, live one's own life.

—Gelett Burgess, *The Romance of the Commonplace*

February 1998

On the low stage, the redhead had our full attention. We'd already seen her spin fire wands and then douse the flame with her lips. We'd seen her wield a bullwhip to snap cigarettes out of the mouth of a leering, rubbery clown in tuxedo and whiteface. Her name was Philomena Bindlestiff, and she was the ringmistress of the Bindlestiff Family Cirkus. The more we saw her, the more we fell in love.

We were at Gargoyle on South Sixth between Berry and Bedford, hard by the Williamsburg Bridge. A bar in a past life, it was now an illegal 'performance space.' It was also hard to miss: a sculpture of a gargoyle jutted into the street over the double doors, blue head and shoulders thrusting over the sidewalk. After a cameo in the Rolling Stones video for 'Anybody Seen My Baby?' the gargoyle had migrated across the river to Williamsburg. If you walked down South Sixth toward the water you saw the head and imagined the monstrous body behind the doors, knees bent, trying to push the rest of the way through. The bridge was so close it threw a grid of shadow over the gargoyle like a *retiarius*'s net.

In November, Rudolph W. 'Rudy' Giuliani had been reelected with almost 60 percent of the vote, and he was using this 'mandate' to squeeze the life out of the city. A former DA, Giuliani treated everyone who disagreed with him like a career criminal. Alongside the continued crackdown on street artists, graffiti, turnstile jumping and marijuana possession, Giuliani unveiled a plan to ban jaywalking. In Manhattan, it could take an hour to cross Fifth Avenue unless you jaywalked, but as the mayor went everywhere in a limo with a police driver, the struggles of pedestrians weren't his particular concern. Under his administration, tens of thousands of people were strip-searched after misdemeanor arrests. Humiliating political demonstrators this way seemed to give Rudy orgasmic pleasure.

One of Giuliani's more ingenious weapons was a seventy-year-old law that banned three or more people dancing in a club or a bar unless the place had a 'cabaret license.' You and two friends moseying around a pool table to 'You Never Even Call Me by My Name'? Verboten. The mayor controlled the Department of Consumer Affairs, which issued, or withheld, cabaret licenses, and bars and clubs were being shut down as fast as patrolmen could scribble citations. In the city that had invented hip-hop, disco and salsa—to name a few—dancing was out.

I'd arrived at Gargoyle that night just before the Cirkus started. A black-and-white film flickered against one wall. In the film, a voluptuous woman, naked except for a Mardi Gras mask, was chained to a bed where she was being tickled with an enormous peacock feather. The film had been looped so it paused on each frame before moving to the next, the woman writhing and giggling in stuttering slow motion. The delay stylized the scene and made the tickling unbearably erotic.

I muscled through the hot, crowded room to the oval bar. Under the high ceilings I could see beds on top of loft platforms. People lived up there, arboreal urban monkeys. For the night, the bar had been restored to its old function: presto, kazaam! Williamsburg loft magic. Forget a cabaret license; Gargoyle didn't have any kind of license at all—not a liquor license, not a fire inspection certificate. The space wasn't even zoned live/work. Super Rudy couldn't be everywhere at once, and so far he'd overlooked the shambles of the Brooklyn waterfront.

Keith Nelson left Hampshire College in Massachusetts with what he would discover were two marketable skills—juggling and fire eating. The juggling he learned from his best friend at school, and he traded a bottle of whiskey for his first lesson in handling flame. Hampshire's hippie utopianism required students to complete a lengthy research project to graduate, something called a 'Div III.' Keith was interested in left politics and wrote to radical groups around the country looking for a Div III internship.

I got the most vague and least promising response from Autonomedia but it felt like the right fit, he says. Autonomedia operated out of a brick warehouse on South Eleventh and Berry and that's how Keith wound up in Williamsburg.

Founded in 1983, Autonomedia published books of the extreme and disturbing, including titles like *The Damned Universe of Charles Fort*, *Whore Carnival* and *Assassination Rhapsody*, 'a pataphysical interpretation of the Warren Report.' Its warehouse had harbored radical publishers since the late nineteenth century and marked the rough border between two mutually uncomprehending Southside populations—Puerto Rican and Hasidic. By the time Keith finished Hampshire in 1990 he knew that New York was the place for him.

I kind of checked in with Autonomedia, he says, and asked them, 'Hey maybe I could start creating a home in the corner of the warehouse.' The answer was yes. The warehouse corner was the cocoon where Keith Nelson began his metamorphosis into Kinko the Clown.

Onstage, Kinko handed Philomena Bindlestiff a long wooden pole and a condom. Philomena popped the condom out of the packet, inflated it with a few puffs and fitted it over one end of the pole. Next she hitched up her spangled tutu and lowered herself to the stage, raising her legs over her head in a yoga pose (Salamba Sarvangasana). She wasn't wearing underwear. No swami had ever done what she did next. As she lay on her back, she inserted the condomed end of the pole in her cunt. (The condom, I assumed, was in case of splinters.) Kinko set a dinner plate spinning on the bare end of the pole and Philomena rolled her hips to keep it spinning, hands free, squinting up from her inverted position. We hollered our appreciation, pressing closer to the stage.

The Gargoyle bartender noticed me with his good eye and took my order. The other eye stared blankly. Someone had told me it was glass and, along with his mussed hair and beard, it made him look perpetually distracted.

Brian Kelly owned and operated Gargoyle. I'd seen him putting up flyers for the show at the L Café. He'd handed me one and said I should come by. Nursing my drink, I scanned the room: I'd arrived solo and wanted to connect. It was still hard to get friends to cross the river. In Manhattan minds,

Williamsburg wasn't a neighborhood, wasn't even a name (but that was changing). My journal from that year is filled with descriptions of brief, troubled affairs, along with complaints about being broke ('I just survived for three days on two dollars,' reads a typical entry). On the wall, the slow-motion tickle continued, arm to leg to breast, excruciating and lovely.

Besides his internship at Autonomedia, Keith landed gigs at the Pyramid Club on Avenue A and at the Blue Angel, an erotic cabaret in TriBeCa. At the Blue Angel, Keith filled breaks between girls with flame manipulation and 'some funky piercing acts.' 'That's when I realized,' Keith says, 'that I could survive by doing variety arts.' In 1992, though, he wasn't surviving on variety arts alone and had to work a graveyard shift as a server at an all-hours restaurant on the Lower East Side. It was there that he met another server, Stephanie Monseu. Stephanie was trained as a jeweler and had spent a lot of time wielding acetylene torches. When she heard that Keith could eat fire, she insisted that he teach her. Flame was the catalyst for Stephanie's transformation into Philomena Bindlestiff.

A low stage had been installed below the wall with the tickle porn and as a spotlight splashed the stage the flickering film stopped. A tall woman with bright red hair stood there: Philomena. I don't remember what she was wearing; I was there as a spectator, not as a recording angel. She was wearing a short spangled black dress, sparkling black top hat and fishnet stockings; or she was wearing a white rhinestone pantsuit, or a black top with black bloomers; or a long white leather coat over white hot pants or a leather bikini; or a tuxedo with bow tie and suspenders. (Kinko's gear tended to be more stable—either loud suits for the showman 'Mr. Pennygaff' or Kinko's hobo-clown attire. Since he wasn't a pretty girl, I didn't pay as much attention to his gear.) Two things I'm sure about—Philomena carried a bullwhip, and she had turquoise eyes.

We started as a fire-eating duo called Fireplay in '94, Keith says. And a year later we expanded to the other performers, moved beyond just fire and renamed ourselves 'Bindlestiff Family Cirkus.'

The new Cirkus had a run at the Charleston in the winter of '96 to '97 and I saw at least one of those early shows with Rebecca, who had a friend living in the Autonomedia building.

Right off the Bedford L stop, the Charleston was one of a very few Williamsburg bars that had survived the post-industrial interregnum. Two belligerent senior citizens ran it—Benny would hit customers with a rolled-up newspaper if they didn't buy enough overpriced drinks, while his wife, Agnes, bragged about how she started there as a dancer. 'We had cage dancers and burlesque,' she said. 'Topless. But tasteful! Not like the filth today.' For Agnes, good taste seemed related to the fact that the dancers weren't allowed to talk to customers (which stymied hooking, I suppose). At the Charleston, pizza was the sole bargain: dollar slices in the tasty, thin-crust Brooklyn style. But the Charleston had the only stage in the neighborhood, and that kept us going back.

What I remember of the earliest Bindlestiff shows is how much they annoyed me. They were painfully quaint. In his white face paint, Kinko made awkward attempts to mimic the patter of a carny barker. His stunts often went wrong, juggled pins bouncing off the stage into the seats. He reminded me of a teenage magician at an eight-year-old's birthday party, not a master of the variety arts. One night someone rode an oversize tricycle around in circles and the show ended with a conga line blundering across the floor. At the Charleston, the Bindlestiffs looked like what they were—art-school kids screwing around.

I didn't understand that the Cirkus was a work in progress, that Stephanie and Keith were learning on the job. Young writers bury their mistakes in notebooks. The Bindlestiffs had to grow up in public. 'At that point we never said no to anybody,' Keith says. 'We took on a mix of the circus variety scene—circus, burlesque, sideshow, drag.' Risk meant the possibility of pathetic failure. I wasn't alone in thinking they sucked. 'They were doing a really lame, children's-type circus when I met them,' Brian Kelly remembers. 'And they evolved before my eyes. Every show they'd get a little better, and a little dirtier. By the time they got to my place it was truly an adult circus.'

That night at Gargoyle each act made a daring bet that the next act would double down. A large man in an electric-blue bunny suit strolled onto the stage and started talking. As his obscene monologue proceeded, he slowly disrobed, revealing a chest as furry as his suit. I knew the Blue Bunny as Scotty, a very gay L waiter who would grip my hand lovingly when I paid my bill. He was followed by a small man, no, a woman with a long silky beard. The woman took a lightbulb from her pocket, put it in a plastic bag, dropped it onto the stage and crushed it underfoot. After picking up the bag and opening it, she put a shard into her mouth and began to chew. Through her mic, we could hear every crunch.

'I saw the best minds of my generation destroyed / by madness . . .' she chanted (crunch, crunch).

'. . . starving, hysterical, naked . . .' (crunch, crunch, crunch).

'. . . dragging themselves through the negro streets at dawn . . .' (crunch).

Her assault on 'Howl' ended with the last masticated bit of bulb, someplace around 'who let themselves be fucked in the ass by saintly / motorcyclists, and screamed with joy . . .'

I'd seen Jennifer Miller on Bedford, often in a black suit, which, along with the beard, made her look like a slim Hasidic man. She also lived in the Autonomedia building. During her stint as a lesbian and downtown singer, my friend Julia had made out a few times with Jennifer. Earlier that year Drew Lichtenstein had married Jennifer's sister.

Between the other acts, Mistress Philomena plied the bullwhip and snapped cigarettes out of Kinko's mouth. No fire marshal would have approved what the Bindlestiffs did next, not in that dusty cave. They juggled fire back and forth before extinguishing it with wet mouths. Flame blossomed in a cone from Kinko's head, making him elemental, a creature of flame. The Bindlestiffs had changed so much from the Charleston shows that it took me a while to realize they were the same people. The mousy brunette who'd flubbed handstands had become a brassy redhead seven feet tall. The irritating art-school clown had become a leering, licentious fool, making us laugh, drawing us in, alluring and repulsing. Kinko also shoved a two-foot rapier down his throat.

An hour into the show, the Blue Bunny and Kinko carried a box onto the stage. The box wasn't large, 3 x 3 possibly, something to crate a microwave oven or a hundred LPs. The men struggled to haul the box, even though Scotty was a heavyweight (which made it mildly frightening when he took my hand at the L. He decided when I got it back.) They placed the box in the middle of the stage and left. A few seconds later we watched as the lid popped open and a nude man emerged, a whispered 'Holy shit' audible in the silence. I couldn't believe a body had been folded into such a small space, a blanket made of flesh. The shock went deep: all through childhood I'd had nightmares of being buried alive or sucked down to the drain of a pool, unable to move or breathe. I'd wake up panting. Now my nightmare was being acted out right in front of me. As the contortionist, Tim, addressed us, casually nude, he splayed his body impossibly, hooking a foot behind his head while standing. Then he did a split that ended with his feet touching over his head.

Tim took a metal wire and, as he described his trip to New York from New Orleans, calmly inserted the wire into his urethra. The wire was a good six inches long but it disappeared almost completely up the length of the shaft. After a few minutes of this excruciation he bent over and pulled the wire out with his teeth.

A mission statement describes the Bindlestiff Family Cirkus as 'a non-profit performing arts organization dedicated to increasing the knowledge, understanding, and appreciation of the history of circus, sideshow, vaudeville, and related arts through activities including performances, lectures, print media, and workshops for the general public . . .' The statement is accurate enough, but it completely misses what made the Bindlestiffs such high-octane voodoo in 1998. It leaves out the fire eating, the sword swallowing, the hollow-dicked contortionist and the bearded lady with her lightbulb recitation.

How had they done it—gone from slumming college kids to dirty angels? Practice and more practice, sure. But there was more going on. The Bindlestiffs had tapped something in the pulse of the city that Mayor Giuliani was trying to stifle. They were physical historians digging into the past and making it live. Academics blow dust from fossils, but artists can resurrect them. The past the Bindlestiffs explored was one of sideshow, freak show, carny, the place where America went to gape at folk virtuosity and genetic deformity.

The carny tradition was nearly dead when the Bindlestiffs went looking for it. Movies killed vaudeville and burlesque and TV poured dirt on the corpses. Carny had always been louche: Come get drunk and stare at the freaks! Ogle the showgirl as the sadist tosses knives at her tits! Blow your hard-earned cash trying to win stuffed animals for your date! It was something America outgrew—we were cleaner, healthier, better than that.

Every July, the Giglio Feast was celebrated outside the Shrine Church of Our Lady of Mount Carmel on North Eighth. Italians on the Northside had emigrated primarily from the city of Nola, near Naples. The Nolani had their 'giglio' (*gigli* = lily); they had their patron saint, San Paolino, with his miracles and a competition in his honor that climaxed with townsmen shouldering a fifty-foot-high wooden shrine through the streets. A facsimile shrine had been built for the Northside, and Nolani immigrants carried it down Driggs Avenue during the saint's procession. By the 1990s the porters had aged and thickened and their sons had moved to distant cities and married non-Nolani wives and it was obvious that some year soon the tradition would come to an end, you hoped before old men dropped the shrine and pulverized a bloc of spectators. Even in decline the lifting astonished—the men grunting and marching, rimed with sweat from summer and strain, a drum corps hammering rhythm to the martial dance.

New World rituals accessorize the feast in a three-week street fair. A maze of tin trailers with orthographically challenged signs (**HEY** "*How's Your*" *Braciole*) housed grade-school dropouts and various bluff ethnics who tried to separate you from your cash. That year the street fair had a dunking pool where a clown dared you to toss softballs at a target and put him in the water. 'High and dry!' he would shout as we tossed softballs at the target, amplified voice reflecting off trailers all down the concourse. 'High and dry!' with an evil cackle that I could hear at my desk two blocks away. A sign on one trailer proclaimed: 'World's Smallest Woman!' I paid the barker and went inside to find an African American dwarf in her fifties sitting on a couch in front of a television. 'Hello,' she said wearily and turned back to the TV, only a gray Afro visible above the couch. I left as fast as I could. You couldn't stare at freaks; deformity had been elided from American life.

The Bindlestiffs brought geeks back. Philomena and Kinko had squirmed into a despised tradition and suppressed their gag reflexes, shaking off middle-class preoccupations with taste and disgust. In Williamsburg the Cirkus showed us that carny still worked. There was life in those traditions, something primal and gross. I'd seen 'performance art' in the city that crossed some of the lines that the Bindlestiffs did. At a show at Limelight in Chelsea, I watched people in fetish gear tenderly abuse each other. In one bare room an Asian woman in a leather catsuit preened in front of a naked man tied to a crucifix. She drove twenty needles into his chest and then hoisted him into the air with wires attached to the needles. At Limelight and in the dwarf trailer, I was a voyeur. The Bindlestiffs were different. They were like us. Their mix of transgression and play wasn't something we recoiled from: we embraced it. We were leering at freaks and admiring fellow artists—the Bangkok Ping-Pong ball routine had turned bohemian. Up close we could see the strain and tension, the risks they took. In a city that was being reconstructed in plastic from Times Square to South Street Seaport, they sweat and bled.

The Cirkus put us in touch with our bodies. When Philomena and Kinko were in front of us, we couldn't push bodies away. Bodies did things that were ugly and remarkable; bodies were often depressing and disgusting, but they were alive. On television, it's hard to see how professional athletes have anything to do with you. In slow motion and from dozens of camera angles they're antiseptic—they're machines, cyborgs, avatars, rockets. The closest we can get to those heroes is an arena with sixty thousand other worshippers. Pressed up to our faces, the Bindlestiffs put us in touch with what bodies suffered and could do. That was why we loved them.

Napoleon II

Hey, Napoleon, the waiter said.

What's up, Matt? Napoleon said.

Napoleon was sitting at the L Café. After his first visit he'd gravitated to the back hallway where a few tables pressed against the wall opposite a payphone and the bathrooms. An old iron lighting bracket and a random painting provided décor. Napoleon liked it there, because Southside instincts made him feel exposed in the main room and because he wanted to keep a low profile—as low as you could with waist-length dreads. He usually came in late after he closed his barbershop. All the waiters knew his name.

So I'm having a party at my place, Matt said. On Friday night. I was hoping you could come by.

Sure, Napoleon said. I'd love to.

Matt scrawled his name and address on a napkin. It was the first time Napoleon been invited to a party by one of the neighborhood artist types. (An actor, Matt would later perform with Blue Man Group.)

When Napoleon showed up for the party with a bottle of Absolut, he wasn't sure he'd gotten the address right. It was a warehouse on a deserted stretch of North Fourth between Berry and Wythe. He saw the lights on an upper floor and the last name on the buzzer. The door opened and Napoleon handed Matt the bottle. Matt slapped him on the back and brought him upstairs.

Napoleon had been to plenty of parties but this one meant something different.

I was just glad that somebody extended that friendship, he says. I thought to myself: I'm in. I was almost into the whole clique, the whole scene.

Napoleon never applied to the High School of Art and Design, but his fashion sense remained avant-garde. On the Southside, he was one of the first kids to sport the hip-hop look. 'I had my six fronts,' he says. 'Eighteen carat. Mostly I wore Ralph Lauren and Guess, Tommy Hilfiger and Polo boots. I even had Cuban links for a while.'

A key element to the look was the 'fade' haircut, an

'aggressively tight taper,' hair clipped close on the sides and back and 'fading' up to almost any length. In the late eighties the fade came to define hip-hop culture and became rococo in its variations and distortions—bald fades, Caesar fades, the flattop, the Brooklyn fade, along with symbols, names and numbers, everything from stars to lightning bolts blazoned into the scalp. For barbers, the fade proved lucrative, as it had to be retouched every week, but it was a hard cut to learn, and styles became more exotic and geometrically rigorous.

The first time I ever saw a fade, Napoleon says, was in Harlem when I was maybe ten. These kids had dollar signs in their hair and I was like, 'Wow, how did they get that?'

A few years later when Napoleon started getting his fade, he had to make a long commute every Saturday to a barber shop near Kings County Hospital. Sometimes hours would pass before the barber, Red, summoned him to the chair. While he waited, Napoleon watched the way Red sculpted the look. When it was his turn, Napoleon had questions.

I asked him, Napoleon says, 'How did you learn this?' He told me, 'You just take your time. Go slow. Whenever you're here, watch me.'

When Napoleon went back the next week for a touchup, Red gave him a running narration—how to hold the clippers, at what point to change the half-inch attachment for the one-inch, when to pull off the collar and use a straight razor and shaving cream on the nape. Week by week, Red tutored Napoleon in the art of the fade.

Still, Napoleon's knowledge remained abstract: he needed a lab rat to experiment on. Opportunity presented itself in another cousin, this one fresh off the island. Napoleon felt bad for Eddie and his country ways and tried to show him how it was done in America. He'd tell people in the neighborhood, 'This is my cousin. I know he's a little weird, a little awkward, a little slow, but he's all right. Don't mess with him.' He told Eddie what to wear and how to avoid getting punked.

Immigrant parsimony meant Eddie was too cheap to take care of his fade. Instead of a flattop, he had a 'fat top.'

It was horrible, Napoleon says.

Seeing his chance, Napoleon borrowed a pair of clippers from some girls who lived in his building and told Eddie he could take care of the fat top. Eddie got nervous but Napoleon reassured him. He could cut hair. Red had taught him. It would be no problem. Eddie said, 'Okay. Let's do it.'

He was so gullible, Napoleon says.

The next day, kids on the block came up to Napoleon and asked him if he'd cut Eddie's hair. Napoleon thought they were going to make fun of him.

I must have done a pretty good job, he says. Because they were like, 'Oh, can you cut mine?' I told them I wasn't a barber but they said, 'Just try it. Do that fade thing that's popular.' If you had a fade in my neighborhood back then you were considered the rebel kid. All the other kids' moms would say, 'Oh, look at him with that fade!'

Napoleon went to work. At first he cut in his bedroom but hair got into everything. So he moved to the bathroom, which did not go over well with his sister. The next stop was the living room but his mom wasn't pleased with that. He wound up in the hallway next to the elevator, where there was an electrical outlet. The super complained but Napoleon ignored him. With his customer perched on a speaker box, Napoleon would sit in a little chair and buzz away. It was his mother who finally had enough of the doorbell ringing and the neighbors bitching. She sent Napoleon to the old barber on South Third between Keap and Havemeyer. Napoleon and the barber made a deal.

I knew another guy, Napoleon says, who was cutting hair at home like me. I told him, 'Look, dude, I'm going to start working at this barbershop. Do you want to get down?' And we made some flyers, and it worked out.

By the time he started cutting fades, Napoleon had already abandoned his. As a kid in the seventies, he'd sported a big 'fro, at least until his father returned from the DR, where he lived part of the year. Then it was off to the barbershop. 'I'd just see clumps of hair falling down,' Napoleon says. 'At the end I looked like a balloon. All shiny.' In high school he gave up the gangster look to grow his hair out again. First he tried Jheri-curling it, 'which was a bad mistake,' then he had a ponytail. 'It was long and bushy. I'd gel it up and by two o'clock in the afternoon it was all puffed up. Out of control.' Dreading gave him the solution. Long hair made for problems in the neighborhood, though. For one thing, it was different from other kids' styles. For another, the mane made it impossible to find work.

Every time I tried getting a job at a store, Napoleon says, they were like, 'Sure. But you got to cut your hair.' So I was like, 'All right. Thanks. But I'm not cutting my hair.' Owning a barbershop meant never having to get a haircut.

Napoleon's shop was the first on the Southside to do fades, and the business grew at Mach speed. By the second year, Napoleon would walk in at ten in the morning and not leave until after midnight. He charged ten dollars a cut.

I had guys come in saying, 'How many you got next?' 'I got fifteen and five more coming later on.' So they'll go to the clubs and they'll come back and I'm still in the barbershop. But by then I'm so exhausted. They'll go, 'Yo, can you please cut my hair?' I was like, 'Naw, man.' But then I'm like, 'You know what? Okay.' At that point all I saw was ten dollars.

If you're a good barber, Napoleon says, you never sit down. No breaks, either: he'd eat a banana, slurp a carton of OJ and keep working. When the line backed up, he'd put on his Walkman, turn up the drum and bass, and cut fifty, sixty heads a day or more. 'Once I cut seven dudes in an hour,' he says. Still he couldn't keep up with the demand.

You didn't want too many guys waiting, Napoleon says. The guys coming in would see and ask, 'How many you got next?' 'I got nine.' 'Shit.' Too much testosterone and guys who want to get back to their girlfriends and play at the court or whatever, so you want to keep these guys moving and flowing.

Napoleon had customers coming in from uptown, from the Bronx and Queens. He even had two guys travel all the way from Pennsylvania every month. Then one day: disaster.

I was cutting on a Saturday, Napoleon says, and all of a sudden my wrist locked up. I was like, 'Oh shit. This is painful.' So I finished the haircut and closed the shop. For the next three days, I couldn't even get a quarter out of my pocket.

Napoleon had already been thinking about a change—he was bored of cutting hair, not to mention that standing up all day was destroying his body: sore feet, backache, stiff neck. Carpal tunnel was a catalyst to try something new. He sold the barbershop to a friend and began to research his idea for another business, something he felt Williamsburg was finally ready for.

The Northside? The painter sneered. You live on the Northside? She looked me up and down.

Where are your piercings? she said. Where are your tattoos?

Just the earrings, I said, not sure how to defend myself. I knew what she meant, though.

I hate the Northside, she said.

But my place is really cheap, I said as a fallback. Five forty a month. So I can afford to live alone.

I guess that's okay, she said, somewhat mollified.

After Rebecca moved out, I decided that my rent was too high and tried to find a cheaper option; I found sticker shock. Kenn Firpo informed me that I couldn't get a Northside one-bedroom for under nine hundred. A year later that number was over a thousand. I could have lived with roommates, but after a lover, roommates were a step backward. So I hung on at 147.

The painter and I were sitting at the Gargoyle bar a few weeks after the Cirkus performance. Candlelight barely reached the walls, making the big room a cave. A few other people talked in the shadows and a Doberman wandered around, pressing your hip and wiggling before moving on. It wore a collar of artificial pearls. The stools were too low for the bar so I felt like a child, barely able to rest my elbows on the wood.

I had only a faint understanding of the painter's Northside contempt but she saw the changes more clearly than I did. The Northside wasn't a freak haven anymore; it had become cool.

Don't worry about me, she said. I'm a total alcoholic. I mean, look at me. I dress like a bag lady.

I looked at her, a chunky girl under thirty with a snub nose on a broad, tanned face. And yes, her sundress with its stains and rips could have been snagged from a Dumpster.

Our faces were thirteen inches apart but she was shouting. Her name was Lily.

I actually make a living from my work, she said. I make lamps that are quite amazing. I sell them at street fairs. Light interests me. I'm very interested in light—backlight and top light. Have you ever held up a mandarin orange slice to the light? It's amazing. You can see every vessel, every drop of fluid.

At the Bindlestiff show, Brian had told me he ran Gargoyle as a club on weekends. He told me that there was no point in showing up before midnight. So I arrived at one a.m. with a buzz on. The sixteen-block traverse took me down gray Southside streets, a place where you could still walk into trouble. The only color came from the bodegas, Latin men drinking in fluorescent light, salsa rolling through open doors. The old bank buildings on Broadway loomed over us, ruins of imperium.

At Gargoyle, I'd started talking to a handsome mixed-race guy named Karl. He slurped down a vodka tonic in seconds and ordered another—he seemed desperately anxious. He told me that he was a writer but I soon learned that he was a costume and prop manager for film. Writing was something he hoped to do, someday. Lily heard us talking and jumped in—she was a writer too. But then again she wasn't.

I make lamps, Lily said.

Brian Kelly moved to Williamsburg in 1982 for one reason—it was cheap. A Pittsburgh native, he'd found himself priced out of Manhattan. His cold-water loft above a Hasidic mirror shop on South Eighth and Roebling cost $350 a month, and it was huge, over two thousand square feet, more than big enough for Brian to build the sets he designed for TV shows, commercials and theater. The loft had one drawback—he couldn't make it warm. 'My heat was a woodstove,' Brian says, 'and it needed constant feeding. I'd scour the neighborhood for pallets that I would cut up and feed to the monster.' When Brian couldn't meet the woodstove's demands he put up a tent and crawled inside. 'That's how I made it through the winter, just me in the tent with a space heater, a television and a tiny bed.'

The loft straddled the eastern edge of the Southside, where Latin and Hasidic lived together with a universe between them. On Broadway wig shops shared walls with *pollo asado* restaurants. Cross Broadway north and you'd find green plantains and merengue. Two blocks south and you shared the sidewalk with men wearing *shtreimels*. Blink and the world went from color to black-and-white.

I make all kinds of lamps, Lily said. I just sold this one with a rabbit bursting through a brick wall. It has 'Hope' written on the shade. I do this other one of a cowboy, he's shooting, 'Pow! Pow!'

She crooked her hand into a gun and pumped air bullets through my chest.

Over the cowboy's head, she said, is a sign that says, 'Neurotic.' That's why he's squinched up like this and 'Pow! Pow!' People on the street see me pushing my cart and think I'm a bag lady. They feel bad for me and try to give me money.

She leaned even closer, exhaling a spittle mist. I didn't pull away; we were drunk and the warm spray felt intimate. Lily was obnoxious but not cruel. Obnoxious I didn't mind.

Anybody want to buy some pot? a voice said. We turned

to a teenager, dusky and thin, Nuyorican or Dominican (he would have said 'Spanish'). Karl lit up. He hadn't said a word since Lily had blitzed the conversation.

How much? Karl said, and then: Is it good?

Karl and the kid went into a huddle. Lily kept talking. She told me that she was British and in the States on a dead visa. Two of her lampshades rested on the bar. The gilded pieces looked like they'd grown on a coral reef, broken loose in a storm and floated to shore.

Those are beautiful, I said. Do you have a gallery?

I'd learned this was a question that you asked artists. I hadn't learned that it was a question you didn't ask artists who might not have a gallery.

A gallery is the last thing I want, she said with the same contempt that she'd used on 'Northside.'

Galleries charge so much money that only rich people can buy your stuff. I sell my lampshades at flea markets, for twelve or twenty dollars, to regular people. An old Italian lady bought two last Saturday. She didn't care that they were art or important or whatever. She just liked them because they're beautiful.

I nodded. I was friends with a very pretty young artist on the other side of the river who told me there was no difference between art and design, between the *Mona Lisa* and hand-screened wallpaper. She bragged about all the art parties she went to and how Harmony Korine spied into her bedroom from his apartment across the street. Both Lily and the pretty artist were snobs, but I liked Lily's snobbery better. It was Williamsburg snobbery.

Karl came back to the bar, arm around the Spanish kid.

Did your man take care of me? Karl said. He seemed worried. He said it again: Did your man take care of me?

In his first eight or nine years on the Southside, Brian didn't go out much.

You could buy crack on every other corner, Brian says. And at night sitting on the roof you would hear gunshots. I never got bothered, though. It was a quiet little hamlet.

There just wasn't a lot to do: life and work went on in Manhattan. Then the Right Bank opened on Kent and South Eighth (in 1990) and became his neighborhood bar. Brian made sure to be there on Wednesday nights when Vic Thrill got outrageous. The smaller the crowd, Brian says, the crazier Vic was. By the early nineties, as Brian felt more at home, he had the idea to start an 'auction club' in Williamsburg.

A crowd would be coming into a giant toy box, Brian says, and the things would be around the room. They would bid on them silently so I could decide whether to let them go for that price.

The first auctions took place at the derelict Kings County Bank on Broadway. To find his artifacts, Brian would trawl the outer boroughs and beyond.

My partner and I would go around to those warehouse auctions, he says. Go out to Jersey for garage sales on a snowy day where you can get things for a song. I'd bring them home and, well, put a lick of paint on something or fix something, make it sellable.

Brian also hosted the first party at the former bank, a Halloween show called 'Fright Bank' that featured thirty installations from local artists. After a falling-out with the woman who bought the building, Brian used the money from the Rolling Stones video to relocate to South Sixth Street. The gargoyle tagged along.

Do you think I should sell my stuff on the Northside? Lily said. To those pierced people?

She considered this.

What I might do, she said, is go up there with a briefcase and whisper, 'Hey, come over here. I want to show you something.'

Gargoyle had been converted into living quarters by way of unpainted Sheetrock and imagination. The gloom made it hard to tell how many bedrooms Gargoyle had or how many people lived there. Those rude lofts messed with my sense of space. I grew up in a land of houses—houses with living rooms and kitchens, not a land of twenty-foot ceilings, ad-hoc closets and beds you reached on ladders. Even after two trips to the Gargoyle bathroom, I still needed directions to find it. Williamsburg lofts were changing the way I thought about home.

Lily vanished and I looked around, noticing for the first time that every surface was covered with curios—glassware, LPs, lamps, a bronze martini shaker, clothes, doll furniture. Price tags hung from the curios; Gargoyle was prepped for sale. As I lifted a deco ashtray, I realized that I was being scouted by an older Spanish guy. His hair curled over his shoulders in greasy strands and cotton rags wreathed his body. The Puerto Rican mummy made a decision and took the bar stool next to me.

I started drinking at six a.m., he said. The problem is that I'm on the night shift. My factory makes boxes. Corrugated boxes. I can't say it's the greatest job in the world, but they treat me right. The real problem is going home. I'm so tired I can't stay awake long enough for my stop on the train and I end up in Canarsie. Or like this morning when I felt like having a few beers afterwards and that's how I ended up in this place.

Joey had grown up in a nearby tenement his father owned. His father had just sold the building but, Joey said, 'I still have a bed there.' Joey had the nasal accent of the Williamsburg native. He invited me for a bump and we went into a back room. I leaned over to sniff and waited until the rocket went off under my feet and lifted me into the thermosphere. As we walked back to the bar, Joey stretched out his arms to the room.

I'm so open! he said.

Most of the other partyers were open—their curiosity and eagerness made me feel like I was around children, lost boys and girls. Poor Joey would have been eighty-sixed out of most Manhattan bars but in Gargoyle his antics went unnoticed. A few minutes after I went back to the bar, I heard his violent whine from across the room, 'Take my picture! Take my picture with the girls!' The Spanish guys and the artists had flown so far outside the mainstream that their orbits touched in the Southside badlands. Alcoholism wasn't the only thing they had in common. As one of a few straight white males in the room, I felt marginal. For a change, I was the square—a colonial administrator paying a visit to a native tribe, a tribe led by the shamans of the Bindlestiff Family Cirkus. Behind the bar, Brian had donned a gorilla mask and gave you two (or three) for one on drinks. Brian controlled Joey's outbursts with a steady hand on Joey's shoulder and soft words.

At Gargoyle, Brian ran the auction club until he realized that auction nights were turning into auction parties, and that partying in his loft was more fun than going to estate sales in the hinterlands. His first big party came soon after Princess Diana's death. He called it 'Lady Di's Rise from the Dead Halloween Key Party.' Guests were instructed to 'Come as Your Favorite Dead Celebrity or as Paparazzi.'

The place got crammed, Brian says. I mean it just got crammed. I dressed like Elton John and sang 'The Bitch Is Back' on the bar.

The role of Diana, princess of Wales, was played by an inflatable porno doll seated on a barber chair/throne.

I rigged her hand to a string, Brian says. So I could pull it and she would wave the royal wave.

There was a cake too.

Lady Di's success encouraged Brian to have more parties and to showcase performers—hip-hop one week, poets another, the Bindlestiffs the week after that. The neighborhood had no shortage of artists looking for a venue. 'I would go around putting up posters,' Brian says. 'Handmade posters. This was even before I had a computer. I'd make them on my little word processor and draw in the artwork.' Just before Brian started Gargoyle, a pirate radio station called Radio Free Williamsburg had moved into the space upstairs. They promoted shows together—a live broadcast from the club and people going up- and downstairs. Despite the size and noise of the parties, Brian managed to avoid a bust.

The cops would always come on the wrong day, Brian says. They would come either the following day or the day before. But they never seemed to come on the day I was having the party!

Brian's major concern was structural.

I worried that the floor would collapse, Brian says. Especially when the place was packed and people were dancing. It was just a wooden floor, plywood, and if you went underneath it was all held up by these stilts in the basement.

My Gargoyle nights blur in a haze of drinking that confuses story lines. A dapper man in tight pants introduces me to his wife, a Portuguese dancer with a sweet simian face (with her low hairline and wide, thin-lipped mouth, she looked like Joan Didion). We dance, her body light in my arms. I watch her making out with a Frenchman who looks like a hippie Gerard Depardieu. The Frenchman explains that the husband is gay, the union a green-card fiction. I can't understand why the husband seems so proud of the marriage, the way he flashes his ring. I don't know anyone but somehow they make me feel at home. A man is sitting in an easy chair, not moving for the hours that I'm there. I think he's asleep but his eyes are open, fixed on the wall. Babble spills over white lines on a tabletop. Moving like she's at a rave for thousands, a pretty Thai girl dances alone to house music. Her hard-faced girlfriend shoots uneasy glances at the rest of us. My last image of Gargoyle is of Brian on the low stage. He's leaning back in the barber chair/throne, the pearl-collared Doberman at his feet. Brian still wears the gorilla mask, King of Misfit Island.

Outside a party in San Francisco in 1991, I ended up sharing a stoop with a bunch of smokers. We were near the Haight and, yes, it was a cold summer night. SF is Manhattan-dense but back then it was friendlier—we could crawl from party to party, addresses on paper shreds in our pockets. Feeling a half-pint of Old Crow, I said—loudly—'I'm so tired of middle-class kids trying to look like white trash.' The kids with their tattoos, wifebeaters and metal T's didn't like my observation and a shoving match ensued. I thought white-trash chic was a West Coast affectation, and maybe it started there, but by 1998 the look had moved to New York.

'Hipster.' It's an old word, and over the years it's meant all kinds of things to all kinds of people, from Dizzy Gillespie to *VICE* magazine. On the Northside it meant a steady infiltration of those tattoos and beaters along with hip-hop stylings, thrift-store grunge, sideburns, egghead sweater vests and round specs from the 1950s. All of it coalesced in my backyard, the old word retrofitted for a new aesthetic.

The new 'hipster' was more attitude than style—the clothes, and the facial hair, would change, but the attitude endured. This attitude involved a very specific type of irony. For the new hipster, enthusiasm about anything 'serious' was forbidden. This applied especially to what used to be called high culture and connected to a deep American leveling instinct, one Alexis de Tocqueville noticed a couple of centuries ago. It was perfectly okay for a hipster to declare his devotion to, say, *Gilligan's Island* and discuss the plot points of an episode with a scholar's authority. *Gilligan* was awful, everybody, even the Skipper, knew it and that made *Gilligan* a perfect subject for enthusiasm—you could be enthusiastic as long as your enthusiasm was ridiculous. I remember walking down Berry Street after a party with a successful poet (as successful as a poet can be—he'd been a Stegner Fellow at Stanford, his poems were published in *The New Yorker*). I showed him a copy of Lucretius that I'd picked up. Now, I wasn't in school, I didn't have a fellowship anywhere, but I loved books; I was hoping for insight or at least a conversation. The poet casually micturated on my enthusiasm. 'Kind of pretentious to have that book,' he said. 'Don't you think?' I left *De rerum natura* at home after that.

The poet wasn't the only one. Another Williamsburg friend had a hipster success with art. He didn't make the art—his dog did. Jason had devised a way to get his dog to scratch and chew on colored Con-Tact paper laid over some kind of canvas. Pull the paper away from the scratch-and-chew and you had a painting. You could buy the paintings at the dog's Chelsea gallery. I turned on Letterman one night and was very surprised to see Jason sitting in the guest chair, dog in his lap. As Letterman cackled, the dog did some action painting right there for the studio audience.

Pabst Blue Ribbon beer was the hipster brew of choice. Any bar that opened in Williamsburg dedicated a tap to PBR. The red-white-and-blue cans filled refrigerators at every loft party. It made no sense—we were drowning in the Great American Beer Renaissance; we had the Brooklyn Brewery right there on North Eleventh. In every bodega, Polish beer was as cheap as PBR and incomparably better, and yet my comrades preferred to drink Miller Brewing Company embalming fluid because working stiffs drank it in Akron back when cars still sported tail fins.

Drinking PBR parodied what the Bindlestiffs were doing with their embrace of sideshow, carny and burlesque. We all wanted to be part of something authentic, and authentic meant outside the American mainstream. It could be a new trend that hadn't been absorbed. It could be a relic that had disappeared from mass memory. It could be a souvenir from some faraway place where the natives had never heard of Coca-Cola, or if they had, they worshipped it, not realizing that the bubbles rotted their teeth.

No sixty-year-old accountant in Scarsdale was going to mess around with carny or PBR: they were outdated and in bad taste. Both the hipster and the Bindlestiffs embraced bad taste, but there was a big difference between them—the hipster rolled his eyes over his aluminum can. PBR was safe. PBR was safe and sideshow was one risk after another. The first was a lifestyle, the second a life. The Bindlestiffs didn't use quotation marks as a safety net. Williamsburg was separating into two different worlds: one the world of the artist, the other subtly different, the world of the artist's simulacrum, the hipster. Often the division split the same person. I sported beaters in warm weather. I wore a baseball cap and had a mechanic's jacket with 'Darryl' on the name tag. But I couldn't be ironic about writing; I was gambling my life on it.

The rise of the hipster was closely related to the phenomenon that had priced Northside apartments into the ether. In light of what came after—the stolen election, the wars in Iraq and Afghanistan, the real estate bubble—it's hard to remember the headline event of 1998 and 1999. The years are prematurely antiquated, a scene in fin-de-siècle sepia. Try to remember if you can reach that far back: it was called 'dot-com.'

I first noticed dot-com when it improved my standard of living. Suddenly I was making excellent money for jobs I didn't know how to do—legal assistant, 'print-lane manager' at Bear Stearns, researcher at the *Silicon Alley Reporter* and writer at other magazines that popped up like psilocybin in shit. Barnes & Noble hired me to read obscure nineteenth-century novels and write synopses of them for an online database.* All these places paid what was to me crazy money: a thousand bucks for a one-page piece about salsa, eight hundred for a four-hundred-word book review—eight bills

---

*I got fired when they caught me adding fantastic details to the synopses (I gave people twelve fingers, Nobel Prizes and dramatic suicides). Apparently, Barnes & Noble didn't appreciate the tribute to Jorge Luis Borges.

for a book review! And it wasn't just the wages, it was how open everyone was to new ideas. Even the editor who didn't buy my story about karaoke gangsters in Ridgewood wanted the one about an Upper West Side dominatrix. There were always more editors at new magazines, young editors intoxicated with start-up money, floating on the bubble. In San Francisco, at twenty-three, I'd survived on a thousand dollars a month—and managed to save—because my rent was only two forty. In dot-com New York I was getting *Vanity Fair* word rates while paying Williamsburg rent. It was the first tangible link I'd ever felt between a $13 trillion economy and my own well-being.

It took me a while to connect dot-com to the changes in Williamsburg. Every other day I'd walk by some cobwebbed storefront and hear the racket of hammers and the whine of circular saws, sawdust golden in the air. A bar and a restaurant opened on my block in the same week with a nightclub on the way. For the most part I liked the changes: Why shouldn't there be ten bars instead of three? A little competition would teach old Bennie at the Charleston not to charge eight bucks for a watery rum and Coke. There were more loft parties and they had better feng shui. I didn't find dot-com folks all that different from me: sure they were a few years younger and they talked too much about their computers, but they made decent neighbors and hey, I liked *Neuromancer* too. The L train was getting crowded and there were more tourists but they didn't get in my way except on the rare night I had to wait for a table at Planet Thailand.

One other Bedford bar besides the Charleston had survived the Williamsburg interregnum: the Turkey's Nest Tavern, still kicking in its second century. Across the street from the Turkey's Nest spread the playing fields of McCarren—

softball on asphalt, baseball on grass, handball and tennis courts (Poles loved tennis) and a football field with goal-posts and bleachers where I played a lot of soccer and skinned my knees on the rough pitch. In New York, location is destiny, and so the Turkey's Nest was a sports bar. That meant eight wide-screen TVs and loud guys in team jerseys bellowing on the sidewalk. One night outside the bar, two Dominican teenagers walked by me.

Damn, one of them said as he looked around. There's mad white people here.

'White' meant something different in Brooklyn than it did on the U.S. Census. There were ethnic neighbor-hoods, still, in Brooklyn that had folks of the Caucasian persuasion—Italians in Bensonhurst, Hasids in Sunset Park, even Irish in the southwest corner of Park Slope. Those va-rieties of white people weren't the 'mad white people' the kid meant. Italians weren't white to him, they were Ital-ians; the Hasids weren't white, they were weird and biblical; even the Irish—and what's whiter than a melanin-deficient Irishman?—were a bunch of feisty drunks. No, white people, the *real* white people, were something and somewhere else, denatured creatures who occupied the suburbs and blurred across TV screens. Culture and social class mattered as much as skin tone. 'White' included chubby guys with olive skin who worked at Bear Stearns and told you they were third-generation Nuyoricans, and you couldn't believe it because they acted so damn white. That was the color two Domini-can kids strolling by on a Friday night could see so clearly.

On March 28, 1998, a Friday, the Bindlestiff Family Cirkus performed at the Brooklyn Brewery, as they'd been doing every Friday for two months. The Brooklyn Brewery had started making beer in an old brewery in Utica in 1987 but only moved operations to Brooklyn in 1996, when the owners acquired a former matzo-ball factory on North Eleventh between Berry and Wythe. I didn't mind having brewery tours three blocks from my house or the fresh product that appeared at places like Galapagos and the Ale House. Besides making excellent beer (the Monster Ale, a barley wine, is their masterpiece), the Brooklyn Brewery 'gave back' to the neighborhood, hosting an annual street fair and the Bindlestiffs's weekly show. On March 28, admission was half off if you dressed like a clown. Clowns filled the room, and the room was full—several hundred people crowding the brewery hall, the biggest event I'd ever been to in Williamsburg.

The Cirkus had a rotating cast, and that night the show opened with a trapeze act. Like tattoos, the trapeze was another castoff piece of carny picked up by bohemia. Sadly, the contortionist didn't appear. Scotty the Blue Bunny got naked at Gargoyle—at the brewery he topped himself by emptying bottles of Guinness over his head as he disrobed, brown fluid and foam running down his chest. Then Philomena and Kinko took the floor. In his shabby tux and white face paint, Kinko looked like a hobo Jack the Ripper. That night he slashed cigarettes from Philomena's mouth with the whip and then, on stilts, ate fire. He also tapped a six-inch nail up one nostril with a small hammer. Philomena juggled fire batons. She was wearing a leather mask, and bright red hair streamed down her shoulders. After the fire eating she poured broken glass from a sack onto a large plastic tarp, took off her stacked heels and lit the torches again. We waited for the next marvel. Philomena commanded the space, a slutastic superhuman Amazon. Both the Bindlestiffs and the neighborhood were getting bigger, and the energy pulled in the rest of the city.

Eli Hormann went to that Bindlestiff show after a solid week of work as a bike messenger. March was a good month for messengers, as ice no longer booby-trapped the roads but summer heat remained far away. Hormann had moved to New York from Boston after college and drifted until he wound up in Williamsburg. While working unsteadily, he managed to get evicted, along with his girlfriend, from a Southside loft in 1995. Eviction implies conflict, and when Hormann saw the agent of his eviction, one Paige Stevenson, at the show, he decided to express his anger. It's surprising that he recognized Stevenson at all, since she was dressed like a clown. As they yelled through the din of the performance, Stevenson's boyfriend, Drew Feuer, appeared. Feuer had just finished a second-shift gig as a crewman on a Hudson River tugboat. No matter what your idea of a tug man is, I bet it doesn't look anything like the compact Feuer, who had dreadlocks, abundant piercings and a bestiary of tattoos, including a dragon that curled around his neck. Feuer saw Hormann and knew what was happening—he'd been around for the eviction. Shouting evolved into punching. Then the six-foot-four Hormann threw the five-foot-six Feuer to the floor and started kicking him with steel-toe boots. The crowd broke up the first round, but there weren't bouncers to toss them out—this was Williamsburg, we didn't need bouncers. They went back to fighting and Feuer ended up on the floor again. Hormann may have been on the verge of smashing Feuer's head against the concrete floor, or the crowd may have restrained Hormann—reports differ. Where nobody disagrees is that Feuer whipped out a Leatherman pocket tool and stabbed Hormann three times in the chest and stomach. In court months later, Feuer said that Hormann's blows were particularly painful because of his facial piercings. He said he was sure that Hormann was going to kill him.

We were waiting for Philomena Bindlestiff to walk across the highway of broken glass when a space cleared around me and I found Hormann at my feet. A woman crouched and took his hand. His breath came in shuddering gasps. I'd heard that anguished sound before, after a steering wheel crushed a friend's chest in a car accident. Hormann's shirt was pulled up to his throat. Blood patched his skin and drops of blood speckled the floor. I had no idea what was wrong with him: Maybe he was really drunk and fell on broken glass. Maybe he'd had a seizure. Why is his shirt like that? Sirens ripped through the Brewery windows, moving closer. I wondered if someone had reported the Bindlestiffs for fire code violations.

The lights came up and Philomena took the microphone.

That's it folks, she said. Show's over.

I was still thinking that we'd been busted for an illegal show. I didn't move. Hormann's face was a gray I'd never seen before, and it turned grayer with each second. Stentorian breaths spasmed his body but the breath faded, then stopped. When two burly firemen walked past me, I finally connected the body to the sirens. One fireman knelt next to Hormann and fumbled with a black case. The second took Hormann's wrist. Then he patted Hormann's cheek.

Hey, guy, he said.

I noticed a dent in his thermoplastic helmet. Mistress Philomena shouted into the microphone.

Show's over, folks! she said. Go home!

The firemen were still fumbling with the oxygen mask when I left. I was blocks away from my apartment but no way was I going home. So I kept walking, just one of the people leaving the show and adding to the ever-growing crowds on the streets of the Northside.

At least one blow from the Leatherman punctured Eli Hormann's left ventricle, pushing blood into his chest cavity. When blood filled his chest it squeezed his heart so that it couldn't beat. That's why there wasn't much blood on the floor or a visible wound. Without oxygen, Hormann's other organs shut down, including his brain. When I read about the attack, I had a vision of dark blood, blood pressing, strangling a heart.

I joined some friends at the Brooklyn Alehouse. We talked excitedly about the stabbing. The windows were open and spring excited us as much as what we'd seen. A small man festooned with tattoos walked up to our table and told his story.

I was holding his arms! he said. I saw the whole thing. I was holding his arms when he stabbed the other dude! Then he ran away.

He left us and wandered through the bar inflated with his story, talking to anyone who would listen.

It would be a few days before the full details came out. Paramedics had revived Hormann but he was in a coma after major heart surgery. Ten weeks later he died, on June 11—his second death—without regaining consciousness. A grand jury dismissed the charges against Feuer but a second grand jury, two years later, found him guilty of manslaughter in 2000.*

*Feuer appealed and the Appellate Division reversed his conviction in 2004.

The Altamont of Williamsburg, someone called it. Nothing like that had happened in the neighborhood. There'd been shootings, stabbings, rapes and robberies, but we didn't do it to each other. I didn't know what to make of Hormann's death. It made Williamsburg feel less like a village. The city was taking us back.

4

The Sleepwalkers

1999–2003

My date with Kelly started at the ghetto movie theater on Broadway under the elevated J-M-Z tracks. The movie was *Fight Club* and there were fewer than nine people in the theater, including us. Although the soiled floor hugged my shoes like Krazy Glue, I maneuvered my leg against Kelly's. After the movie we went to Diner, which had opened that year on Broadway and Berry. Diner operated in a seventy-two-year-old railroad car that tilted sharply toward the river. The car had been renovated but not too much—the mosaic floor was scarred and the vinyl-topped counter stools swayed. A mirrored panel behind the counter duplicated our every move.

We drank kamikazes that night; at least I can still taste the sweet bitterness of lime. While we drank, the pretty waitress and the pretty bartender danced to 'Spoon' by Cibo Matto. Every time I went into Diner the women were dancing together to the same song, happy and young, making the party fun. Diner was a long walk from North Eighth Street but I'd added it to my neighborhood. Planet Thailand and Veracruz tried too hard, but Diner was chic, a retro-cool Manhattan outpost. Two other 'diners' had just opened, Miss Williamsburg on Kent between North Third and Metro, and Relish on Wythe between North Third and Fourth. I didn't think any of the diners would have pleased Lily but I couldn't ask her. When Brian couldn't make rent on Gargoyle, he sold his lease.

Kelly and I had gone to college at the same time, drifted apart and then run into each other again that summer of 1999. We were two writers over thirty who drank heavily and hadn't published much. Although she'd been a fantastic actress in college, Kelly had picked writing and was on the verge of finishing her first novel. College baby fat had melted away to reveal an elegantly beautiful woman. We circled closer over the summer, closer every time we met, but nothing happened. That night at Diner, I told a crude joke and Kelly said, 'That's why I'm never going to sleep with you.' She kept repeating the line. I took it as an indication that she was thinking about sleeping with me.

We weaved onto Broadway laughing and brushing against each other. On South First I couldn't stand it anymore and I shoved Kelly against the iron fence around Saints Peter and Paul Church. Kelly jabbed her fingernails into my throat but I caught her wrists and held them over her head against the fence rails. I kissed her. She bit my lip, then kissed me back. We stumbled into the church gateway where stained-glass Peter and Paul looked sternly down. Caught up in lust, we didn't register the shouting. I finally turned to be blinded by a flashlight.

What are you doing there?

I squinted: the light and voice came from a large van

that had pulled up next to us. The van was NYPD white and blue.

What do you think we're doing? I said.

Kelly stepped in.

I'm okay, she said. Everything is okay.

I looked into the van. There were at least eight cops inside, faces against the window like kids on a junior high field trip.

Well, it doesn't look good, the cop said. You better go home now.

We walked away. I was furious. Even more, I was bewildered. In five years in Williamsburg, not one police officer had addressed a single word to me. I never saw cops walking a beat or squad cars patrolling—not when I ran in the park at midnight, not when I walked on the waterfront alone. Cops didn't show up when you got jumped. Cops didn't investigate burglaries. This was poor, ethnic Brooklyn and you were on your own. The trade-off was that the cops didn't bother you. And now here they were, scolding me for kissing a girl. Dad had come back from the suburbs. Williamsburg was in play.

Kelly and I walked a few more blocks, then fell onto a bench at a bus kiosk and went back to grappling. I threaded my hand under her white blouse—no bra—and gripped a nipple. She bit through my lip; I tasted blood. We were going to get along. Then the van rolled up and the flashlight blinded us again.

I thought we told you to go home, the voice said.

I jumped off the bench, sputtering curses. Kelly grabbed my shoulder and jerked me back.

Calm fucking down, she said, keeping me from doing . . . well, nothing much. Yelling at the cops for a few minutes before they cuffed me and carted me away.

Take me home, Kelly said.

She led me to where she was house-sitting, a loft on North First. The loft was on the top floor of a warehouse, a pauper's penthouse, and belonged to a dancer, another old classmate of ours. There was no bed, just views of the bridge and the rutilant Manhattan sky. Kelly lit candles and I remember her putting down blankets and us lying on the floor. What happened next was much nicer than a night in a 94th Precinct holding cell.

Sundays washed me up at the L, where I'd sift through the wreckage of the weekend. My adventure with Kelly had made the month but substance abuse was dunning me with the usual toll. The L still did good business early but by the afternoon it was half-empty. I'd gather abandoned sections of the *Times* and sit for hours pretending that this hungover Sunday I was going to do some writing. Other weekend survivors clutched the tables and drank the ghastly coffee, their eyes ringed like bandits.

Kelly and I hit thirty and then thirty-one and thirty-two and everything had stayed pretty much the same. She was working a secretary job at Lord & Taylor. I'd traded the T-shirts and sawdust of carpentry for the jacket and tie of a 'legal assistant' and a succession of freelance magazine gigs. The more I saw of men's magazines, the less I wanted to, but the offices were slightly less disgusting than law firms, those multistory cash registers. Kelly felt the same way: no upward scramble as a well-dressed bitch at Lord & Taylor for her, no matter how good she looked in a pencil skirt. We took those jobs because they were easy to get and they didn't follow us home.

Even so, we were older than the folks doing the same jobs at adjoining desks, only a few years older but we could feel it. Some of the hotshot editors and execs were younger than us, too—they were making high five and low six figures and getting married and buying prewar one-bedrooms on the Upper East Side. Kelly had no fixed address and me, I lived in a shanty and my office oxfords came courtesy of the Salvation Army. It had been almost ten years since I'd left college and except for an ineffectual agent, I had nothing to show.

Kelly and I were holding out for something better. Everything else had disappointed us but writing never could. With writing it was always your fault. So Kelly rewrote the opening scene of her novel a hundred times. So I worked on the first novel for six years before I showed it to anyone. We held on and watched the neighborhood change around us.

On the other side of the L, a man who looked like William S. Burroughs—same spectral face with the same hatchet folds—kept smacking his book on the table and sighing noisily. The explosion finally came.

You're ruining my book! he shouted at Barista Jim.

Jim, and everyone else in the room, stared at him.

This goddamn music is ruining my book! Burroughs shouted, and slammed the book one more time.

The music was loud and punk, which made sense because Jim was in a punk band—and wore his shredded biker jacket as he worked the counter. Jim was also a diabetic and a junkie (there were so many junkies in Williamsburg).

We watched Burroughs stand up, screw the top off the honey jar and dump honey on the tabletop. It took a while

151

but nobody spoke or moved. Burroughs waited for the slow puddle to spread, threw a bunch of coins in the mess and ran out the door.

Forty-some feet below us, the L station was getting a face-lift. A work crew on ladders and scaffolds slathered paint on the girders and ceiling and swabbed the wall tiles. The rollers dappled their orange reflective MTA vests and headgear and they insulted each other in English and Spanish. From shit brown and peeling to bright red and green—in the future, you would step off the train at the Bedford stop into perpetual Christmas.

I gave up on the *Times* and tried to figure out how much I'd earned writing. It was the perfect way to get even more depressed. The play that had led me to Rose had also earned a $5,000 fellowship from the state of New York. Even with that score, and adding all the $15 reviews and $40 articles, the number I came up with was under $15,000—for a decade of work. A good chunk of the money had come just that year, writing for start-ups, but it still wasn't close to a survival wage. The confidence that had launched me out of college was fraying. My novel, *Fellow Traveler*—the reason for my vow of poverty—had crawled across the desk of every editor in the city and died. Every time I read a first book, I looked at the bio to see when the author had published it: twenty-six for D. H. Lawrence, twenty-five for Joyce, twenty-eight for Kerouac. Wallace Stevens didn't publish *Harmonium* until he was forty-four but he was a poet, and he also had a really good day job.

Maybe, a voice whispered, all the confidence is a delusion.

For Kelly our affair was an interlude, a vacation from a rough couple of years. When I met her, she was involved with a (married) advertising executive who had drug and pornography addictions, not to mention two kids. She'd met him at a strip club, which should have told her something (she bartended there but he'd lured her into the 'champagne room'). When he got a job in Seattle, she followed him across the country. The exec lied about his late-night disappearances and when she got pregnant, he pressured her to have an abortion. She did. Then she moved back to New York and out to Williamsburg. But double-barbed hooks still ripped her heart; I was ten feet down the block from the loft on our first night when the ad exec pulled up in a black town car.

Four months later the exec overdosed at a party and died. ('They were all strangers,' Kelly said. 'He was alone.' That seemed to make her grief more terrible.) Bohemians aren't the only ones with death wishes. In his will he left Kelly half of his life insurance policy, a quarter of a million dollars. She and I had already split up.

By 1999 the Northside was changing so fast that every trip down Bedford made my head swivel. 'When did that get here?' Or, 'When did that place close?' Or, 'What was that place before . . . ?' A mini-mall with the 'New Brooklyn' vibe—yoga, art books, Tibetan curios, vinyl—had opened in the Real Form girdle factory on Bedford between North Fourth and Fifth. It was owned by a member of the Hasidic Satmar sect. Satmar proselytes parked their 'Mitzvah Tank' in front of the alterna-mall and men dressed like Abraham

Lincoln ambushed you on the corner and politely asked if you were Jewish. Cop to it and they'd invite you for dinner at the Chabad House upstairs. Black Betty, the neighborhood's first real lounge, had opened in the badlands at Metropolitan and Havemeyer. Planet Thailand had left its tiny storefront on Bedford between North Seventh and Eighth for a palace on the Berry side of the same block. The new Planet Thai had a DJ, art exhibits, a sushi bar, a hibachi grill and nightclub lighting.

Yet the L Café remained, and so did Frank, King of the Northside Bums. Frank still sat on top of a newspaper box throne across from the L and regarded the café like a cathedral gargoyle forced to look at a rose window until the end of days. He hated Dan, the L owner, but they were joined in Williamsburg antiquity. The ever-growing crowds leaving the subway streamed between the L and the gaunt figure.

'I'm a bum,' Frank snarled. We did not dispute his claim and kept our distance, his pungent body odor as much appanage to his title as hemophilia was for the Romanovs. Frank's reign involuted down to a past that preceded my arrival on the scene and is therefore dim to me. His own stories shed little light as they were larded with exaggeration. He told me that he'd stolen a tank from the National Guard base at the Brooklyn Navy Yard and driven it down Kent Street, 'and they sent like twenty cop cars and army helicopters after us.'

While pretenders arose to challenge Frank, none of them displaced him, not the junkie who supported his habit by stealing L tip jars, not the woman who slathered the schizophrenic plank of her face in Kabuki white and wandered the Salvation Army aisles informing young shoppers that they were whores. Frank was king, troubled, complex, in grave danger, an annoyance to many, a friend to some, capable of secret kindness but always ineluctably there. I'd see Frank at his post on the mornings when I staggered to the subway to make an eight a.m. temp job, and I'd see him there in the afternoon when I returned, and I'd see him at night: roosting on the paper boxes that proliferated on the corner, long legs drawn up, gaunt body hunched forward, there in summer heat and winter freeze. Frank shielded his eyes behind polarized John Lennon specs; the sunglasses dated him, as did his long hair and Zappa fetish. Frank had been in a motorcycle club, the perfect outlet for a Williamsburg rebel in 1970. He still had the motorcycle, a Harley with a black gas tank. In his old-school helmet—no visor—he looked like the last Vandal when he roared down Bedford.

In my early Northside days I'd see Frank on the corner with a black dude who wore Sly Stone super-spade shades and a shirtless Viking in overalls with a red beard about three feet long. Time denuded Frank of companions and he faded from biker to bum. On his paper box perch he was an elongated, squawking crow, greasy hair hanging over his grooved face and drooping black moustache. The moustache so defined him that when he shaved it his face was naked, as exposed as Frank on those nights when he slumped at the L counter and proudly begged for a place to sleep. He ogled pretty girls, he chatted with Polish old-timers; he kept watch.

Give me a couple of thousand dollars, Frank said, and I'll make that fat Dan bastard disappear.

Frank bragged at the L counter, basking in the tolerance of his favorite baristas. The fact that Frank was most charming and helpful to those baristas who were pretty and kind, well, aren't we all?

Oh, Frank, the barista said, Dan's not that bad.

The barista could have been tiny, acid Wendy or sweet blond Sara with her Minnesota accent or Josh, whose stoner vibe concealed an ambitious filmmaker.

By tomorrow morning, Frank said, he'll be just a bunch of bleached white bones and by tomorrow afternoon they'll be a bunch of powder. You know Darling International? They buy bones. The make them into soaps and lotion and bone meal for dogs. So there'll be a lot of dogs eating that fat Jew bastard.

Frank was educated enough to know that 'fat Jew bastard' and Holocaust powder crossed every imaginable line, but he was weak; nihilism was all he had left.

Artists owned the L, a husband and wife: Dan and Pam, as they were known to customers and staff. He was a musician and producer; she had a dance company. Outside the café we could have been friends—we would have talked about jazz and how tough it is to sustain a dance career. I would have listened to Dan's CDs. At the L, no big spender, I was the enemy.

Dan floated over the L floor, insubstantial for such a large man. Even when scolding the staff, his voice never rose above a mellow drone. He leaned over barista shoulders, re-arranging cutlery and piling napkins. Only the anal pucker of his lips showed the strain.

Being the boss forces a boss identity on you and it didn't suit Dan. If a boss isn't in control, the workers sense it. They snarl and whine; they cheat and steal. This made Dan even more uptight. Dan was an artist and his artist soul shrank from the burden of power. A strong boss can get away with being an asshole—the workers hate him but they fear him. Dan was just hated. He made tense, irrational decisions to assert himself. He'd micromanage for days, then vanish for a week. He fired staff for petty vices like snacking behind the counter (five years after quitting, poor stoner Josh bolted his food for fear of a Dan over his shoulder). Meanwhile other staff members plundered the till and guzzled Dan's liquor, all the while feeling stridently self-righteous. They were striking blows against the machine! They were giving it to The Man!

As for me, I sat in the L but I was not of the L. I was a regular, yes, content to loaf over my bottomless cup of foul coffee, but for years I kept my distance. The waiters were generally kind and I tipped what I could; they were as broke as me. Beautiful waitresses came and went—a dancer with more energy than Con Ed, a rosy pair of English twins, the Polish Italian local, Jen, with her dark blond hair and crooked, sexy smile. Jen had grown up in Greenpoint and her neighborhood friends would gather at the counter and bat around local gossip like the sex-abuse scandal at St. Cecilia's. Word on Graham Avenue was that priests were playing a game called 'lick tongues' with altar boys.

Jen complained about 'counter trolls,' those customers who squatted at the counter and treated the staff like a combination of best friend, eye candy and therapist. Another waiter, the gay, sardonic Jeff, referred to them as TWs, or 'time wasters.' I went to the L five days a week; I did not want to be known as a TW or counter troll. By sitting quietly, by laughing at barista jokes, I made friends. I didn't talk about my problems; they told me about theirs. My elevation over counter troll was ratified when I started getting free coffee—and later, much wine and beer. The baristas let me stay after closing and I kept writing as they flipped chairs onto tables.

The L was launched by a musician, one Kitty Shapiro, in 1992. When I showed up in the neighborhood, the L had the Bedford café monopoly. All it had to do to make money was open.

By 2000, that had changed. Where the chatter of foreign tourists had strafed the atmosphere, you heard only the mumbled complaint of a neighborhood junkie. In the quiet you noticed how grungy the L was—the filthy linoleum on the floors peeling, the walls painted hideous shades of orange and yellow. The pedestrian art exhibits hung forever, the ceilings were too high and upstairs, the neighbors sounded like they were playing Yak Bushkazi. Even the waiters seemed less like charming rogues and more like sociopaths (stoned, angry sociopaths).

Competition knocked the L backward. Café Read, for example, had opened a block away. One wall at Read was filled with good books. The other wall was exposed brick. Read was in it to win it: they even baked their own pastries. It was a better version of your living room. Two doors down from the L was the vegan/vegetarian Bliss. Their bowls of quinoa and seaweed made the L's veggie burger a pathetic gesture.

Dan's disappearances to work on music, absences that went unnoticed when the L had the monopoly on coffee and cookies, became a void as the margins tightened. A dearth of options had made the L the community center but that community was splintering. I'd hung out in cafés and diners across the country. Some of them had been in place for forty years. Grit was part of the charm, like at Macondo on Six-teenth Street in San Francisco with its hippie residue: the paintings had been on the walls there since the 1970s—you could tell by the Day-Glo color schemes under the film of dust, prices taped to the frames long ago in impossible opti-mism. But the L had gone from cutting edge to obsolescence as fast as floppy discs.

Next door, Veracruz suffered a similar decline. Veracruz was the first restaurant in Williamsburg that dimmed the lights and offered cotton napkins. The food was standard-issue Tex-Mex but because it was all we had, we celebrated the margaritas and fried ice cream. Then five other bar/ restaurants opened and suddenly we weren't dying for heart-attack nachos and lukewarm burritos.

I get ahead of myself: in 2000 the L death spiral was still at its widest gyre. The L didn't just turn belly to the wolves, either; it fought for life. The café went restaurant, offering shepherd's pie, meat loaf, fish and chips—comfort food was cool about then. It opened a to-go store so slammed with business that it became a barista gulag. Unfortunately, the vampire was drinking his own blood: much of the to-go business was diverted from the mother ship. The music pro-ducer and the dancer were restaurant amateurs, and food-and-hospitality professionals had forded the river. These professionals hired other professionals to crunch numbers and manufacture business plans. They also paid better than grape-picker wages for cooks who didn't, like one L cook, show up to work drunk and stalk waiters with serrated knives.

Dan had never liked us regulars nursing our bottomless cups and getting cozy with the staff, but the squeeze made us villains. We might as well have been blackjacking him and stealing his receipts.

Napoleon III

As soon as the carpal tunnel subsided, Napoleon was back in the barbershop. But he wasn't going to be there for long.

I told myself, Napoleon says, 'I don't want to lose an arm.' Plus, you have to have a steady, Zen-like motion. I have a blade to your throat, you know? You don't want to give guys a bad haircut. Some of those guys were for real. But I already had a plan.

By 1998 the 'artistic types' covered Bedford Avenue like slurry on a potato field. Some of his Southside friends saw the newcomers as a threat but for Napoleon it made the neighborhood more interesting.

I was cool with it, he says. I embraced it. More diversity, more cultures, more backgrounds. It was like SoHo came to me.

Napoleon knew SoHo better than most Southside kids. In SoHo he had a secret identity, one that he took pains to hide from the neighborhood.

I was a Deep House dancer, he says. And I loved the club scene: Octagon, Tunnel, Red Zone, Mars, Sound Factory, Wild Pitch. It was my escape from the neighborhood and all the thugness.

Napoleon slipped out of the neighborhood in disguise: he'd tuck the dreads into a hat and put on baggies or overalls for the walk to the subway. Once on the train, he'd strip down to his dancing gear: a T-shirt, designer jeans and combat boots. In his bag he also carried baby powder to sprinkle on the dance floor so that he wouldn't slip. Safe inside the club womb, he'd dance until morning. Napoleon wasn't the only hood rat making the switch—friends on the scene donned similar camouflage when they ventured out of East New York and Harlem.

In 1998, Williamsburg didn't have dance clubs or lounges. That was where Napoleon saw his opportunity. The incoming artists might have had unusual ideas about dress and deportment but they had the same basic needs as the rest of humanity—as Napoleon puts it, 'a place to eat, a place to drink and a place to live.'

So Napoleon studied the real estate market and started checking out the 'artistic bars.' He discovered that the settlers liked tin ceilings, ''cause everybody's taking off the drop ceiling and shining it up.' He discovered that they loved wooden floors. 'So they're ripping up the linoleum and sanding the floors down.' He discovered that they liked exposed brick and original moldings and settings. Of course they also liked beer—imported beer and craft and microbrews above all. The next step was to find a location.

When Napoleon was a teenager, Dominicans partied at bar/restaurants with live music. One of the most successful clubs was Don Diego on the corner of Havemeyer and Metropolitan (in the seventies, the location had held a Mafia restaurant called HiWay owned by one 'Jimmy the Nap'). When Napoleon was fourteen, a cousin who knew the bouncers at Don Diego would sneak him in. On the weekend the bar showcased bands all the way from the DR and crowds packed the sidewalk. They played merengue, and they played it loud. Napoleon would lean against a vibrating wall and watch the seductions and grinding on the dance floor. Yet by 1998 Don Diego was fading away.

I noticed, Napoleon says, that the water in the lobster tank was lower every time I walked by. Lower, lower, lower. It was dingy as hell and not many people were going in.

But I told myself, 'That would make a great spot for a bar.'

Then the owner of Don Pedro disappeared.

With food still in the oven and glasses on the table, Napoleon says.

He got the landlord's number from the federal marshal's notice taped to the club door and made the call. The space was available.

When he floated his club idea to friends, they thought he was crazy. 'Northside,' they said. Northside had all the action. Nobody would go to a club all the way down on Metropolitan and Havemeyer. Napoleon saw things differently: a lifetime in Williamsburg had inscribed the street plan onto his brain.

I told my friends, he says, it's not all going to be North Seventh and North Sixth. You can't really go further north because of the park. People are going to go to North Fifth, to North Fourth, to North Third. There's no North Second, so Metropolitan, then North First, then Grand Street. And I told people, it's going to go east, it's going to go south, it's going to go all the way around.

Napoleon stood at the corner in front of the shuttered Don Pedro and looked for patterns. What he saw around him were big loft buildings, and artists coming in and out of the buildings. Those artists had to walk a long way to Northside bars and restaurants.

I thought, Napoleon says, if I were them, I would want to hang out somewhere closer. That way, if you do get drunk, you can crawl home and not have to worry about a commute through a shady area. It made sense to me, and I stood by it.

He sold his share of the barbershop to a friend and found a partner in thirty-three-year-old Bud Schmeling.

They'd met at Teddy's, where Schmeling had bartended for years (he also had a master's in English lit and taught at the Consortium for Worker Education). Schmeling put up most of the money and together they watched that money vanish: $4,000 for beer taps, $4,000 for hard liquor, $3,000 for the sound system, over $5,200 for the liquor license and another $2,500 for a 'liquor license expediter' to massage the community board, $15,000 for the security deposit for the kitchen equipment, $2,000 for an accountant to keep the books. Then thousands more for the lumber, the lighting, the paper spray-painted copper for the ceiling—they were going for a Moroccan theme. 'Black Betty' came from the old African American work song and they incorporated under the name 'Dollar Yo Inc.' Napoleon was twenty-five.

Black Betty opened in late March of 1999 and was an immediate all-out, register-ringing, booze-flowing, rump-wagging neighborhood hit. People didn't mind walking those extra blocks for Williamsburg's first take on the lounge experience. I know I didn't: Black Betty jumped onto my short list of weekend destinations. Most bars are boring because the only thing to do there is drink. The point of drinking is to break free, and bar pastimes—the pool table and the video game, the loud rock band—are too passive for total liberation. So you drink even faster, a race to the freedom finish line before you pass out. Dancing is a short-cut to freedom but if you're a white American male you probably need to be half-wrecked before you even consider shuffling your feet. At Black Betty we could dance without paying a door or getting on a train. Enough Southside people came through to keep it from being a complete white-out, and the DJs were eclectic enough to play different styles (true, there wasn't much merengue). We danced shoulder to shoulder and gripped warm thighs under tabletops and went home together. The energy brought attention and the Black Betty name went out across the city. Manhattan folk followed reviews in *New York* and the *Times*, and outerborough people came on the grapevine telegraph. The outsiders made the scene colder but they helped me realize that my own path was taking me into a bigger city. One night a sub-sub-editor screamed at me because her magazine owed me $4,000. When I'd found out that the magazine was bilking other writers, I'd broadcast the fact on media websites. Hence the screaming. She told me that everyone was suffering, that we were in all in this together, but I doubted that she was eating Campbell's. *Icon 'Thought Style'* magazine went out of business soon afterward. All I got from *Icon* were two feature clips I could wave at other editors. Dot-com was in trouble.

For Napoleon, Black Betty was the first move toward a grand vision.

My plan was not just opening one bar, Napoleon says. It was opening ten. Five fingers make a fist. Two fists and then you get something to fight with.

After the ten bars he saw himself moving into liquor distribution so he could supply his bars and the other Williamsburg bars that were popping like fireworks. Black Betty wouldn't stay the same, either. Napoleon wanted it to mirror the clubs that had impressed him in the city. He wanted the doormen in suits. He wanted the red rope and the exclusion of the cheap and badly dressed. Black Betty would be a place where you could bring a date and find magic, liberation from the routine of sunup and sundown.

The Other Frank

A second Frank was there to usher in the L's final days.

Mutt! the waiter shouted. You got something that you want to say to me? You fuck! You ratfuck. You ratfuck! You gotta say something! Something!

Frank Versace dropped to his knees and stared at the ceiling. We'd seen the movie and knew he was addressing a Jesus Christ visible only to him.

You fuck, you fucking stand there and you want me to do every fucking thing! Where were you? Where the hell were you? I'm sorry. I'm so sorry! I did so many bad things.

The L had closed an hour earlier but locking the front door had only started the party. I sat with the kitchen crew at the counter and we raced through six-packs as Frank and the waitress, Leah, made desultory efforts to clean and the barista, Wendy, sifted through checks.

I try to do the right thing, Frank said. But I'm weak. I'm too fucking weak. I need you to help me! Help me! Forgive me, Father!

We were all watching Frank. We were always watching Frank as he straddled the line between daring and catastrophe. I'd never seen someone so out of control functioning at the same time. On a few nights I'd harnessed the same reckless magic but for Frank it was daily life. Frank would keep a mimosa at the ready on the counter and get so drunk on the job he slurred and staggered but he still efficiently waited tables; he'd grown up in his father's restaurant, so slinging hash was in Frank's DNA. I wasn't the only one fascinated: Frank was the L Adonis. He was sleeping with both of the L managers, and an old girlfriend of his had moved down from Rochester to start a life with him. Some nights all three women would be at the counter while Frank stumbled and weaved among the tables. Two managers as fuck buddies also explained how Frank got away with everything at the L.

That night, Frank and I bulled behind the counter and surrounded Wendy, who, despite and because of her acrid wit, was adorable. She was also about four-eleven and being the stuffing in a manwich intimidated her.

Leah—help, she said.

I'm not getting involved, Leah said. You've been encouraging them.

She looked at us over librarian spectacles. I thought she was jealous. Earlier in the night she'd declared that she was ovulating and that was the only time of the month when she wanted to have sex with Frank. 'I guess we're all just animals,' she'd said.

Wendy wasn't in any real danger. But Frank brought an edge to every encounter, a sense of menace and possibility. He was our bad lieutenant.

Frank had come to the city from Rochester for that old reason: to write. He'd dropped out of SUNY Buffalo after two and a half years but the literary dream took him to, where else, New York City, where he'd landed in a loft on Wooster Street. The loft belonged to the older cousin of a friend who was in Africa. It was the perfect launching point—rent-free!—but as Frank says, 'We fell under some dark forces.' Those forces included relentless partying and heroin. After a friend 'who was actively pursuing the William Burroughs experience' died of an overdose in the loft, Frank went back to Rochester. There Frank started publishing in the small literary scene. A local media mogul had Frank headlining a reading series and got him featured in radio shows and newspaper profiles. 'I was cast as kind of an enfant terrible,' Frank says. By 1999, he felt ready for another attempt on the city.

Friends told him that people were moving to Brooklyn and he found a share in Polish Greenpoint, on Leonard and Norman. 'It was just like moving to a neighborhood in any city,' Frank says. 'Except there was Manhattan.' He didn't consider Brooklyn a destination; it was just the closest he could afford to be near the action. Then the day after he got fired from his Chelsea restaurant job, the phone rang. It was one of the L managers. Frank had put in his application so many weeks earlier that he didn't remember where the place was. The new job brought him into the neighborhood.

That's when I realized there was a major energy coalescing around Williamsburg, Frank says. I saw the concentration of the types of people that were there and I said, 'Oh yeah. This is really where I need to be.'

It wasn't long after he started working at the L that Frank had what he calls his 'explosion,' a loss of control that turned him into the wild creature we watched in the café. If explosion it was, then it happened in slow motion, across a year, and led to 'the breaking of an entire person.' Sifting for clues in the aftermath, Frank had his pick. A car accident that bounced his head off a windshield and knocked him out. Lingering injuries from bare-knuckle boxing matches with his friends and father. Terrible food allergies. Whatever the cause, Frank found himself in constant pain, suffering from blurred vision and blinding headaches. His body became so sensitive that even a paper cut felt like an amputation. He was already drinking heavily—he was a twenty-six-year-old artist after all—but during the 'explosion,' booze and other substances were the only way he could stop the pain.

Despite his physical collapse, Frank kept writing. In twelve-hour jags in his Greenpoint basement, he churned out autobiography and fantasy, from a memoir about working in his dad's chicken restaurant to an eight-hundred-page werewolf novel. In his scrambled life he clung to the idea of being a writer; it was the only buoy that kept him from being just another charmingly deranged ruffian. Despite the hard partying, Frank didn't want to be the next Bukowski; he wanted to be the intellectual's Bukowski: William T. Vollmann. Writing is a business, though, and no matter how dedicated Frank was to his craft, he was too unstable to market himself. Out of control at the L, Frank didn't realize it was no longer enough to live in New York City and write well (if it ever had been). It wasn't an easy lesson to learn; I was still trying to go from an F to a D.

Frank and I became friends a few weeks after 9/11 when we watched a barista lose her mind.

We have to get out of here, Lynn said. Her red-rimmed eyes were wide and fixed and she was sweating.

It was a Friday night around ten p.m. and the L was pretty much empty, a few regulars at the mismatched tables, a European couple holding hands and cooing near the window.

All of you, Lynn said. You have only one life. Shit's gonna come down on us. This is bullshit!

Conviction ran through Lynn's words like rebar. I'd heard her speechifying to the staff all night. Lynn was short and chunky but her eyes were liquid and she moved with an absent sensuality, her thoughts on another world. We were finding out what that other world was.

Bullshit, she repeated. All bullshit.

Frank sidled over and whispered that it had been going on for a week. He was ethnically handsome, black stubble over clear pale skin.

'Jersey boy gone big-city,' I thought.

He side-glanced at Lynn. She kept ranting.

Yesterday, she said, my friend was on the train and they made everyone get off. And they didn't tell them why. Nothing.

She paused to let this sink in.

Why didn't they say anything? she said, then answered her own question. It's because they know something is about to happen, she said. Any day. They have intelligence. They just don't want us to panic. Our lives don't matter. We're sheep to them.

Lynn's voice was even and lucid but the tendons in her neck bulged. A couple of the kitchen people stood at the back door watching her. The L kitchen wasn't in the same building as the café but next door, on the to-go store side. Runners brought plates through the backyard, which also served as a warm-weather 'garden.' The kitchen staff— cook, prep cook, dishwasher—seemed misplaced on a restaurant floor. Their stained whites and sweaty faces made the connection between dinner and slaughter all too visceral.

China is siding with the Taliban, she said, looking back at them.

And China, she said, has nuclear weapons.

I think she's going to crack, Frank said.

None of the customers seemed to notice when Lynn's voice jumped to a yell.

Tonight! she said. It's going to happen tonight!

A jet broke the sound barrier overhead. Since the attack, jet fighters had swept over the city day and night, specks on the blue of afternoon, invisible in the dark, the whistle and crack reminding us of what had happened.

That's it! Lynn shouted. I'm gone!

She ran out from behind the counter, apron flapping, and dashed through the door.

The commotion brought the kitchen folk to the counter.

What's going on? Dave said. He was the head cook (you couldn't really call him a 'chef'). Curly red hair covered Dave from his beard to the backs of his hands. His eyes were a different shade of red, the burst-blood-vessel shade, and he reeked of weed. I realized what had fueled Lynn's paranoia.

She took off, Frank said. She thinks the next attack is on its way. I bet she's headed for her bunker.

Dave didn't find this funny.

This is bad, he said, rubbing his beard. It's very, very bad. She's been predicting all this and now it's coming true.

Dave looked at the door and then headed back toward the kitchen. A minute later he reappeared with a khaki backpack.

I have to check on Karen, he said. Karen was his girlfriend.

The prep cook and a new dishwasher gawked from the back door but didn't make breaks of their own (although neither lingered for an after-shift drink). The next time I went to the L, Dave walked out of the kitchen no more drunk or stoned than usual. Lynn never worked a shift at the L again.

Americans from Christopher Hitchens to President Bush reacted to the attacks exactly like paranoid stoners. Gangsters had broken into the gated community, dragged us out from in front of our TVs and beaten us unconscious. The week after the attack, a friend turned to me and said: 'I didn't know they hated us so much. I had no idea.' But how could she not know? She had a graduate degree and a *New Yorker* subscription. Before the attack what happened outside the gates wasn't real. It was pictures on the TV screen. Then the thugs in their rags and turbans kicked down the door. The old reasons couldn't explain what had happened and there were plenty of crackpots and cynics ready to provide new ones.

Magda

Yo, Robert! the kid said, flashing a gold grill.

He pronounced my name with that guttural Polish upthrust on the second syllable.

I had no idea who he was. In the mini-mall he'd greeted me from one of the padded benches that lined the lobby walls. He had a DIY faux-hawk and his face bristled with metal—a nose ring, a silver gleam on an eyebrow and studs, labrets, rings and a 'flesh tunnel' in the conch, auricle, daith and lobe of his ear. Through shredded layers of clothes, I saw a blot of tattoo ink. Piled around the bench were half a dozen plastic and paper bags stuffed full. He looked like an East Village street urchin but had the smooth red cheeks of a toddler. His eyes were a strange shade of blue.

You don't recognize me? he said. It's Magda.

I couldn't hide my surprise: she'd become a completely different person.

I know, she said. I'm not all the way there yet. But I'm clean and sober. For twenty days.

That's good, I said.

I was back in Bellevue for a while, she said. But they told me I was okay.

Magda hadn't had a sex change, but she'd transformed her identity in the absolute way only a teenager can. And she'd suffered.

It had been over a year since I'd last run into her; she'd lost her model perfection by then but she'd still looked like the same person. She'd told me that she'd been diagnosed with schizophrenia and that she'd be taking meds for the rest of her life. The drugs made her spacey, she said, but they were better than thinking she was both God and Satan and in control of everything that happened—the fall of a leaf, sunset, war in Somalia, every murder and kiss. 'I don't have hallucinations,' she'd told me. 'But every word means a hundred things at once.' She'd said that she was clean then too. Now she was a tough-talking street thug.

I saw that motherfucker Marcin, she said. Right out on the street. He tried to be friendly and I said, 'I should have my boyfriend cap you for what you did to me.' All that bullshit and lying about everything. But I also told him, 'It's the past. So I'm gonna let it go.' You know what else I told him? I said: 'I'm glad you introduced me to heroin.' He's the reason that I'm here today.

Marcin had moved out of the cave in 1999 because Judith was pregnant. A little Goth troll had replaced them. Her Halloween black and orange hair framed a perpetual scowl. She hosted a zoo—a dog, cats, ferrets. Every night death metal, marijuana and the ammoniac reek of urine rose through the floorboards. I missed Marcin.

Magda squirmed off layers down to a white singlet with a lace neck. A roll of fat folded over her belt. She didn't have to starve for beauty anymore.

I have to go to the bathroom, she said. Watch my stuff.

Even though I hadn't seen Magda, my landlady had provided disapproving updates. 'That girl is wicked. She talks to me very filthy. And she is always stealing and taking the drugs. No one trust her.' Mental illness was not a category that Henryka recognized.

Magda skipped back from the bathroom and grabbed my arm.

Robert, she said. It's my eighteenth birthday tomorrow!

Congratulations, I said.

Well, I'm still here, she said. Tomorrow night I'm having a birthday party at Black Betty. You should come. You can meet my lover. We're getting married soon. He gave me my first orgasm. And I've laid a lot of guys.

She looked at me, weighing a thought. Those eyes were the only thing about her that hadn't changed.

Are you rich? she said.

No, I said. Why?

Because then you could buy me a beer.

I went into the Verb and got her a Sierra Nevada. Happy Birthday, Magda.

In the following months, I ran into Magda up and down Bedford but at the L above all. Because the baristas, mostly, tolerated her and because she, mostly, was homeless, she landed there five or six nights a week. She'd waltz into the café with a Fisher-Price tape recorder in one hand, Wu-Tang playing to distortion on the tinny speakers. 'Wu-Tang muthafuckas!' she'd shout and free-form rap. The Wu-Tang Clan were her brothers, she said. They loved her because she was 'black, Polish and African American.' I wondered if she would have gone crazy in another place—supercharged New York had overwhelmed her. She kept getting arrested, once for attempted car theft. 'I was trying to jump-start it with a butter knife,' she said, 'but the cops rolled up.' Her outfits included artifacts from the modeling career—striped silk tie loosely knotted over a white silk blouse, lightweight wool dress pants with holes in the knees, designer cowboy boots. Where once she'd gotten $300 haircuts, her hair jutted up in gummy spikes. She was always kicking dope and she shared her methadone stories. She stopped methadone once for three days 'because I'm so into this guy. And he's so into me!' The happiness pulsing through her body had her bouncing in her chair. But a few days later she stopped talking about the guy and her pupils were shriveled.

Magda was the worst of the counter trolls, treating the L like it was Mommy and she was a three-year-old. She'd bum cigarettes, beg for coffee, steal tips. She'd sleep on the low garden walls no matter the season. It was well below freezing one night when I walked into the garden and saw her dozing there, breath steaming in the air. When she walked in an hour later, she was shaking with cold.

That looks like mine, Sara said, pointing to the brown silk scarf wrapped around Magda's blond head.

It is, Magda said.

On her way out, she grabbed Sara's lit cigarette from the ashtray.

Yet no matter how bad her behavior, Magda didn't get banned from the L, because she was a woman and because she was broken. One of the waitresses let Magda clean up at her apartment and even sleep on the couch. Magda assured the waitress that they could shower together if it would save on the water bill.

I saw Marcin on Bedford, daughter in his arms round, dark-eyed, gurgling. Marcin was wearing khakis and he'd filled out. He looked prosperous. It was as hard as ever to follow the slanting avenues of his conversation—a story that he wanted to do about prostitutes from Kazakhstan and their dangerous pimps, another story about punk rock kids who jousted on bicycles. I did learn that he was shooting for an agency and life was better than good. When I mentioned Magda, he shrugged. 'Heroin can do that to you,' he said. 'Some people are not survivors. I am a survivor.'

Magda still sported the navy pea coat, for warmth and for shoplifting—holes slit in the lining made it the perfect vehicle for boosting. Spoonbill & Sugartown, the high-end bookstore in a mini-mall, was a favorite target (I called it 'Spoonfed & Sugar Tit' because I couldn't afford their titles). If Magda saw me in the mall lobby she'd hawk books to me, even though she was standing outside their door. She'd nap on the mall benches during the cold months, and when they kicked her out at ten she'd migrate to the L. Stumbling down Metropolitan after some party she got hit by a cab and spent a year with a cane, limping and swearing.

Sham was a survivor too. His eighteenth birthday was much healthier than Magda's. When I saw him at my corner bodega, I didn't recognize him either. Man muscle swelled the once gaunt frame. We talked and he told me he lived in Florida with his father. That explained the February tan.

I like it down there, Sham said. You can go to the beach every day. And the girls . . . Wow. I'm back in school now too. Computers.

I didn't do it to help him, Frank the Bum said. I wouldn't piss on him if he was on fire. Unless I could piss gasoline. It was that kid getting stabbed. You see something like that and you need to help out.

Frank the Bum was now Frank the Hero, the man who had foiled a robbery at the L To-Go. A few nights earlier, a homeless desperado had walked into the store at closing and waved a knife at a barista named Dane. Dane had emptied the register but when the desperado grabbed the tip jar, Dane rebelled ('You can have Dan's money, but not mine!'). Dane ran out from behind the counter, wrestled with the robber and received the knife in his ribs. The robber bolted out into the street where—in Frank's version—Frank tackled him and pinned him until the police came. It made me reconsider Frank's stories. Maybe he actually had beaten a Golden Gloves champ in a street fight on Driggs (I still didn't believe the one about the tank).

Frank's turn as crime stopper had brought him new confidence. His strut into the L was more assured, his visits more frequent. He sat for longer and didn't turn down a free cup of coffee; he was the man who had saved the L. A few weeks earlier I'd heard him ask Versace if he could move into his Greenpoint apartment—what a team that would have been—but Frank the Hero had dignity and needed no favors.

For Dan, Frank's intervention was another plague from God. Despite the fact that the bum continued to bad-mouth him, Dan handled the aftermath with grace. No, he said, the barista should never have chased down the thief; no amount of money was worth getting hurt. Yes, they would change procedures around closing, although the door really should have been locked. Dan even managed to thank Frank and Frank responded with humble munificence. The robbery attempt, so dramatic to us spectators at the counter, was a small event in the secret economic life of the L, a life that was rapidly draining away.

The death of the café was measured out in drugs and drink, and in staff delinquency. Restaurant workers always steal and over the years at the L, I saw endless theft. A girl from my hometown worked as a waitress there one summer. She told me that some of her coworkers would write fake checks on stolen pads and then pocket the money. A prep cook filled his backpack with comestibles at the end of shifts for months. When he finally got caught, he became indignant. 'I have a lot of time on my hands now,' he muttered at the Greenpoint Tavern. 'And I'm going to devote it to making Dan miserable.' Word of the threats got back to Dan. 'If I get killed in the next couple of weeks,' he said, 'you'll know who did it.' What made the endgame different was that the theft was so brazen. Sometimes staffers would walk in off the street and grab a six-pack or load up paper bags with wine bottles. Dan and Pam had a child that year, which kept them away from the restaurant, and the managers weren't in any position to maintain order—Sara was a soft touch and Tammy was one of the worst offenders. Even after the collapse of the dot-coms and 9/11, Williamsburg stayed hot—grew hotter, even—and the café was burning down.

It never seems to move, Frank said. But I'll go to the kitchen and when I come back, it's climbed all the way from the bottom to the top.

Maybe it can teleport, Curtis said.

That would be the perfect superpower for a snail, I said.

We were sitting around a sixty-five-gallon aquarium in Frank's bedroom where we'd moved the party after the L closed for the night. The tank held a few plastic rocks, a plastic diver with a three-bolt helmet and bulky suit and exactly two living things—a sprouted scallion bulb and the snail. The snail had latched on to the bulb and its eyestalks undulated in the current.

What does it eat? I said.

That's the great thing, Frank said. It eats the plant. That's all it needs. But it doesn't eat much so the plant is fine.

Frank passed the lightbulb he was holding to Roy. The element had been removed from the bulb. Frank dropped a white crumb into the hollow and clicked a lighter under it. Lips at the bulb top, Roy slurped the curling thread of smoke.

It's an entire ecology in there, Curtis said.

Curtis was Frank's best friend and a habitué of the L counter. The counter had always served as a depot for staff friends and lately Frank's tribe had taken over; it was a groovy place to hang out and watch the Frank Show.

Roy passed the bulb to James.

Aah! James said and dropped the lightbulb into his lap. He blew on his fingers. The glass was hot. It was the first sound James had made since they'd started smoking. James worked in the L kitchen. He was also Frank's flatmate. James's room had two high grilled windows that faced the back staircase. The room was located directly over the boiler for the building. Steam seeped through the cracks and left puddles on the floor. Lacking a bed, James slept on a mound of clothes in the perpetual dark. That morning, Frank had noticed a pencil protruding from a fold in James's belly (James was burly and covered in reddish-gold hair—golden hair, golden beard, furry toes). The pencil had wedged in his bulk during the night. James roamed the kitchen for an hour without dislodging the pencil.

A kitten leapt at my jeans and went to war with the cuffs.

A second kitten jumped on the first and they rolled away. Their mother, enormously pregnant, swayed by and disappeared under a heating vent. The kittens dashed after her.

She's about to pop, Frank said. I made a nest for her under my bed.

They just . . . vanished, Curtis said.

As the bulb circulated, a joint went around in the opposite direction. They'd been smoking joints like Marlboros all night. I knew how strong the herb was—I'd smoked some a few nights earlier with Frank and it had made me feel as anxious and powerful as the God of the Old Testament.

The cats go through the entire house like that, Frank said. They can even get outside. It's their underground railroad.

Like James, Roy hadn't said a word since the lightbulb began to make the rounds. An illustrator and comic artist from Holyoke, Massachusetts, Roy was one of eleven Irish Catholic brothers and sisters. Roy was usually soft-spoken but he always slipped into conversations with witty observations and non sequiturs. The meth muted him. In college I'd once snorted the tiniest line of crystal and spent a sleepless forty-eight hours writing what I considered the greatest work of nonfiction since *The History of the Peloponnesian War*. Turned out that it wasn't, which explained why I didn't hit the pipe. I had a real book to write.

I'd sold a real book proposal to a real publisher and found a real girlfriend. Nadia was a dancer and filmmaker. She didn't drink or use drugs but she tolerated my occasional rampage. What could be better? It felt like growing up. We snuck into McCarren Park Pool one night and the place impressed her so much that she recruited two dancers and shot a video there, the women spinning across fragmented tile.

Nadia said she wanted us to move in together and I agreed—in theory. As much as she appreciated my hovel at 147, she didn't see it as a place for *us*; she wanted a bigger apartment. 'Fine,' I told her. 'If you can find a bigger apartment in Williamsburg I'll move in with you.' That was the same as saying I'd never move in with her, because by 2002 there weren't any bigger apartments in Williamsburg that we could afford.

I was older than everyone on the L staff except the hard-drinking head cook. Five, seven, even ten years older. And it mattered. Watching them, I felt like I was on the stern of a ferry looking over a foam trail at the shore.

For centuries, artists were considered bad company for respectable people. At some point the paradigm flipped and artists started being seen as rich kids sponging off parents to make art that was ridiculous and incomprehensible. The artists at the L came from the older stereotype—Roy's dad worked in a mill and James put up with being steamed alive in a hole because the cheap rent gave him more time for music. Almost everyone at the L had come to the city for the same reasons: to play music or paint or write. Yet it was harder for them than it had been for me. New York had gotten more expensive and rich kids were dangerous competition.

As late night hushed Brooklyn everyone drifted away. Only Curtis said goodbye. He ran a word-processing center at a bank and could afford a cab ride home. That left me and Frank. Frank put on a CD and a guitar avalanche swept out of the speakers.

It's hot in here, Frank said, and took off his shirt. He dropped to his knees in front of the speaker and let the sound waves cool him. In the gloom, his pale body glowed.

He did not look healthy, shoulders hunched, stomach bulging. His room was a writer's room. Books and papers rose in leaning towers around his desk, good books too, Lawrence's *Women in Love*, Genet, William Blake's collected works and numerous thick volumes from our mutual hero, William T. Vollmann. Every page of Vollmann had a brilliant sentence and there were a lot of pages.

Chris III

Like anyone with eyes, Chris saw the changes on Bedford Avenue—the new restaurants, the cafés, the shops. What he noticed above all, though, were the women.

You'd be walking down the street, he says. And you'd look at this gorgeous girl. And she'd look at you! And the two of us would be looking back over our shoulders, staring at each other all the way down the block. And then you'd walk into a telephone pole.

Chris had come a long way from the days when the cuginettes snickered at him on Lorimer Avenue. The changes on the Northside meant that he didn't have to stare forlornly across the river; the city had come to him. Eddie Vedder boots and long hair made him right at home on the new Bedford. Plus Chris had a nuclear option, the weapon every teenage boy dreams of wielding—he was in a band. In fact, not only was he in a band, it was his baby. All across the neighborhood, places were just starting to open where he could showcase that beautiful child. Of course, he had competition, competition of the invasive variety.

The music guys were finding their way here, Chris says. At first I was a little like, 'Who the fuck are you guys? I'm doing the band thing myself over here. This is my world.' But then I started to realize that the audience they brought was there for me too.

Swinger Eight was Chris's band, a trio with forty-year-old Ozzie Martinez on drums and Chris's best friend from college, Chris Medrano, on bass (Medrano's family owned 666 Metropolitan, where he still lives). At the corner of Manhattan and Driggs, Enid's was the first Greenpoint bar ('99) to cater to the settler trade. Past Enid's came the black-out of McCarren Park and Pool. While hanging out there one night, the three men gathered around the Tetris table and made a pact. They were going to stick with Swinger Eight and go as far as the band would take them.

It was totally dumb, Chris says. Three-handed fist and 'Yeah!' But a lot of fun.

In the new venues, rock-and-roll hopefuls played loud and murky for clumps of friends in fetid halls. Chris had been going to Teddy's since he was an underage drinker but relocated to the Stinger Club on Grand and Roebling, where he'd run into Napoleon. 'The Reverend Vince played there every Monday,' Chris says. 'I remember an amazing show where he was naked on the bar with an accordion and a rose between his ass cheeks.' For business, Chris preferred the Mark Bar in Greenpoint because 'that's where a lot of musicians I knew hung out.' Swinger Eight played Trash Bar on Grand and they played Galapagos, the first art space/bar in the neighborhood. Galapagos opened in 1998 in a former mayonnaise factory on North Sixth. Through the metal walkways overhead you could see the old mayonnaise vats. A big reflecting pool at the entrance delighted the drunk and stoned.

We *lived* in Galapagos, Chris says. At first it was more of an art space but then they opened the back room. We ended up getting it whenever we wanted. I'd usually sand-wich us between two bands and do a pretty fair evening. The bar numbers were also good. We knew a lot of drinkers.

I'd gotten to know Chris at the Verb. When we talked he pushed the band; it wasn't a hard sell but he knew I wrote music reviews and I'd end up with the latest Swinger EP. I saw some of those Galapagos shows, Chris standing with his guitar over numerous effects pedals. Chris liked to turn the lights off and run projections on a movie screen while Swinger played long-form trippy shoe-gazer sounds (later the band went metal). While Chris was still writing fiction and comics, they became a sideline. Music had an immedi-acy that writing lacked, not to mention that women pre-ferred guitarist/singers to aspiring novelists.

Another drink? Frank said.

I nodded.

He ducked to open the counter refrigerator and pulled out a bottle of white wine. A cork pop and pour, then Frank topped the glass with a splash of orange juice. At the L, OJ had started as a way to hide alcohol theft and then become a habit. We called this drink the 'Frank.'

Frank came out from behind the counter and waved a broom.

Got to finish this cleaning, he said.

Well, get working, I said.

Working, he slurred. Yeah. Working. That's my thing. Wasting time, that's your thing.

Frank stayed witty even as he slipped into oblivion. It was part of his allure. As he escorted the last customer to the door, he stared at her prominent ass. He turned to me and muttered, 'Do you know what a centaur is?' I only hoped she didn't.

It was Frank's night to close and the rest of the staff had left. They'd left even though Frank was drunk when I walked in at nine o'clock and got drunker as the night stretched on. That's how it went at the café: we swilled Dan's booze at the counter like the L was our private club and stray customers who wandered in were crashers we were too polite to eighty-six.

When Frank had poured my first drink three hours earlier, I said, 'You seem like you've had a head start.' Frank had denied it. 'Not a drop yet,' he said. Of course I thought that he was lying; I saw the way he slouched and veered to the right, exactly like Harpo Marx (it would be years before I found out that it was something more drastic than alcohol). Despite his slouch and slur, Frank managed the tables, made small talk and dropped checks.

Can I give you any help? I said as Frank lifted chairs to tabletops in a prelude to mopping.

No, he said. You just keep writing that great American novel. Writing novels, that's your thing. Pushing this mop, that's my thing.

Buddy, I said. It's not a novel. NON-fiction.

Frank answered with a punch to my shoulder. He might have been stumbling but it hurt, bone bruising muscle.

Uh, ow, I said as I rubbed the impact crater. What the fuck is wrong with you?

'Novel,' he said, was a figure of speech.

That wasn't good enough so I stood up, brushed my palms on my pants legs and hit Frank on his upper arm. He stutter-stepped backward but didn't rub the spot.

There must be mosquitoes in here, he said. I think one just bit me.

He hit me again in the same place. I returned the favor. We glared at each other then Frank rushed forward and pinned me against the wall with a forearm. With his other hand he threw uppercuts into my stomach. I shoved him back and got in a boxing stance, not sure what was happening.

Wait, Frank said, and lifted his hands. We can do this, but we gotta have rules.

Frank wasn't talking like a drunk.

I used to do this with my friends all the time, he said. No punches to the face or below the belt. Everything else is legal.

Okay, I said. It wasn't a proposal I could turn down.

I moved toward Frank but he clinched before I could hit him. We wrestled in the narrow passageway between the counter and wall. The punches went back and forth and we leaned into each other to muffle the blows. Bare-knuckle fighting was different from fighting with gloves (which I knew something about). In the new game, I didn't want to break the rules. Even more, I didn't want Frank to break the rules. One misunderstanding and we'd end up hitting each other in the face. You couldn't trust a crazy man and I wasn't sure Frank was sane.

We knocked back and forth between the wall and counter and reeled out to the floor. Frank would hit me and I'd wobble back as tables and chairs crashed around us. Frank didn't seem to be trying to kill me, so I adjusted my punches: hard but not deadly. I learned the game as it went on. With bare hands you could hold a wrist. You could grab a shirt and pull the other man close. No referee yelled 'Break!' The fight went on. When one of us got tired the other one seized the opportunity to throw combinations—stomach, ribs, shoulders. My glass of Frank dropped and shattered. We ended up wedged in the entrance to the bar, still punching. Frank stumbled into the cash register and it fell to the floor with an iron clank. The credit card machine followed. Menus scattered. Frank was wearing a white button-down shirt. The oxford looked good on Frank, bringing out the contrast between his clear skin and black beard. As our endless round dragged on, I noticed red flecks on the white of the shirt. It explained the raw feeling in my left forearm—when I hit Frank in the body, his belt buckle shredded skin. His knuckles were bleeding too.

Frank started to get sloppy. His punches strayed to my thighs or glanced off my shoulder to my face. I sobered as the fight went on but Frank got more drunk; sweat matted his hair and his eyes glazed. I was afraid that he would hurt me but I didn't know how to stop him. I couldn't quit, and even if I did, I wasn't sure he'd notice.

We brawled back into the corridor next to the counter, scraping a painting from the wall. I broke our grapple, took two steps back and hit Frank in the belly as hard as I could. He collapsed. I stood over him, gasping. His breathing was even and smooth and his eyes were shut. No baby ever slept better.

The café was destroyed. We'd upended half the tables and splintered a chair. Napkins, menus and cutlery scattered across the wet floor. We'd knocked over the cash register, the credit card machine, the schedules and the coffee urn. It was two in the morning: the L would open in four hours. On the floor, Frank dreamed.

I picked up the broom.

Frank, I said.

No answer.

I poked him with the broom handle. I felt like a fisherman who drags a shark onto his boat. The shark is still dangerous—one writhe and it could bite off your arm.

Frank, I said, and poked again. He stirred, waved an arm at the disturbance.

We have to get out of here, I said.

A hand to the floor, a push to his knees, a gathering of senses and Frank was upright. I watched him closely. Frank scanned the room.

Let's get out of here, he said.

We went out to Bedford, dragged the security gate down and kicked the padlocks shut. In all my years at the L, I'd never noticed the iron anchors sunk into the slate blocks outside the café. As we worked, two girls walked by. Lost tourists. They paused, wondering if they should be afraid of us. I didn't blame them.

Watch this, Frank said.

He swaggered up to them. The streetlamp revealed a lunatic. His hair clumped in damp tufts and bloody streaks adorned the white shirt.

Hey there, Frank said. Can I help you with something?

They warmed at his approach. I wanted to warn them.

Um, the taller one said with a simper. We're looking for Black Betty?

She was wearing gold lamé hot pants.

I can tell you guys how to get there, Frank said. You want me to take you?

Well, the shorter said. She'd tied her shirttails together to reveal midriff and cleavage. A lot of cleavage.

The girls exchanged a glance.

I guess so, the taller one said.

The night had gone on long enough for me. I said goodbye.

I stayed away from the café for a few days but finally slunk in. When I sat at the counter, it was the usual hellos as I waited for my coffee. The L's shabby order had been restored. Sara smiled her warm smile before rushing off to bail the sinking ship with a thimble. I wondered if Frank had gotten fired.

It was a full month later before I felt bold enough to bring up the fisticuffs to Sara; we were at the Greenpoint Tavern.

Is that what happened? she said. I couldn't believe it when I walked in.

We weren't in good shape, I said. But we made sure to close the gates.

Sara rolled her eyes. Business as usual at the L. I was relieved but almost offended that I wasn't news. Frank and I had plenty of competition. A bunch of teenagers collectively known as the 'punk rock kids' had taken over the kitchen. They all lived together in the 'punk rock house.' And they hated Dan. Dan's restaurant license was on the wall behind the counter, and someone had drawn a pentagram around Dan's photo and given it horns. A trap in the basement had executed a rat and someone had chalked 'Dan' on the floor next to it. Everyone suspected the punk rock kids but no one confessed. Dan claimed anti-Semitism because it was easier for his ego than anti-Danism. The abuse led Dan to cancel the Christmas party. 'I just can't have a party here when I know my employees feel this way about me.' Sara was fond of Dan, but not even she went along with that. Dan had asked her to buy a partnership in the restaurant, but after a conversation with the restaurant bookkeeper, she declined. She might have been midwestern sweet but she was also midwestern shrewd.

•

Frankie V. gave his two weeks' notice in August of 2003. His last shift brought controversy (surprise, surprise). Someone left a laptop in the café and Frank took it home with him—a parting gift. When the laptop owner called the L, Tammy told her that they had it. Tammy was no longer sleeping with Frank. Frank refused to return the laptop, and it took a threat of legal action to wrest it from his hands. When I asked Frank about the controversy, he went Socratic on me.

It depends how you define 'stealing,' he said. He chose not to test the dialectic in court.

The L closed for renovations the week before Christmas in 2003. It would reopen, we were told, sometime in mid-January. The staff muttered that Dan had scheduled the Christmas shutdown to scuttle the Christmas party for a second year in a row. Mid-January came and went and February too but the security gate remained shut. By then, I had migrated to the Verb. Napoleon had left his hallway table several years earlier for the more refined pleasures of Super-core, a Japanese tapas café on Bedford between South First and South Second. Supercore was always dark and stayed open later than the L ever had. Napoleon would walk in after midnight and sit alone, secure in the darkness. Of course everyone there knew his name.

That Frank the Bum outlived the L Café must have pleased him. After years his application for Section 8 housing went through and he was granted a small apartment on Union Avenue, close to the expressway. No more roosting in doorways. Even with a lock on his door, he couldn't escape the surgeons who gleefully scissored off toes and then half his left foot. Frank won the game of attrition, though, dying in the summer of 2004 before they could make off with a leg. A wake brought several hundred mourners, and a

Frank shrine was erected in the lee of the L subway stair-case, complete with photos, flowers, arts and crafts and testimonials. It lasted through fall and into the winter when rain and snow and wind and ceaseless traffic kicked it apart.

5

Area, Area, Area
2004-2008

That whole territory wherein the Village of Williamsburgh was first established, passed in 1638 from its Indian proprietors to the West India Company for "Eight Fathoms of Duffels, Eight Fathoms of Wampum, Twelve Kettles, Eight Adzs and Eight Axes, with some Knives, Beads, and Awl Blades."

—*Historic Williamsburgh* (privately printed, 1926) by John V. Jewell, president, Williamsburgh Savings Bank

Everything belongs to me because I am poor.

—Jack Kerouac, *Visions of Cody*

On May 11, 2005, the New York City Council approved a blueprint for the Greenpoint-Williamsburg waterfront. The plan rezoned 175 blocks over 350 acres from 'industrial' to 'mixed use.' 'Mixed use' meant that housing could be built there; the proposal suggested that 10,000 units would be added. The devil is fond of small print and he made a home in the clauses that described the intended housing—most of it over a half-million dollars a unit. The original plan offered enticements to developers if they voluntarily designated a percentage of housing for low- and middle-income families. 'Contextual heights' were included for new buildings inland but the sky was the limit on the waterfront: 350 feet, or about thirty stories. To help us gag down ten thousand luxury units, the proposal included candy—fifty-four acres of parks and the promise of public waterfront access from developers, should they feel like granting it.

The city council voted 49–1 in favor of the proposal. Williamsburg was wide open.

Harry Havemeyer ended his 1987 book about his sugar baron ancestors with a prophecy. 'Much of the Eastern District might be called an area in transition,' he wrote. 'It is today at the nadir of a curve. There are large amounts of land to develop both on the waterfront and inland. When will the next entrepreneurs come along? The space and the labor are as available today as they were in 1850. Will the cycle repeat itself? Only time will tell.'

The cycle repeated itself. Mayor Michael Bloomberg cared about the passage of the Greenpoint-Williamsburg proposal. After a career at Salomon Brothers, Bloomberg had founded Bloomberg LP (it was a 'limited partnership' because he owned 82 percent of it), a financial news and information services media company. Bloomberg LP made its first billions from software the company developed and sold to investment banks. The software gave banks an edge on the market. With his company prospering, Bloomberg turned to politics, running as an independent against the reformist Democrat Mark Green. Bloomberg's victory over

Green in the chaotic weeks after the towers fell came as a surprise to many, although the fact that he spent $56 million more than Green should have tempered the surprise. Bloomberg also had the endorsement of the 9/11 hero Rudy Giuliani, who had begged the city to ignore term limits and let him run again.

Bloomberg accepted exactly one dollar a year for his mayoral services; since that made him an altruist, the city council hurried to rubber-stamp all his plans. New York City had made the International Olympic Committee's short list for the 2012 Summer Games and the Brooklyn waterfront was one of the attractions the city dangled before the committee. A new Olympic Village would rise on the East River.

The neighborhood that would house the ten thousand units wasn't as sure about the Olympics or the mayor's altruism. On December 6, 2004, Williamsburg's Community Board I, directed by seven Hasidic rabbis, had voted 'No' on all but one of the city's proposals. The community board had already floated a proposal of its own for the waterfront, one that offered more lower-income housing, more industrial zones and more parks (in 2003, the city council had approved this proposal). On January 13, Brooklyn borough president Marty Markowitz had also voted 'No' on the Bloomberg plan. The councilman who represented much of the district, David Yassky, had vowed on April 4 to spearhead opposition to the plan unless major changes were made. We even had Jane Jacobs in our corner, still fighting at the age of eighty-seven. From Toronto, she addressed a letter to Bloomberg. 'Even the presumed beneficiaries of this misuse of governmental powers, the developers and financiers of luxury towers, may not benefit,' she wrote.

'Misused environments are not good long-term economic bets.'

The mayor brushed us all aside. Less than a month later, the City Council Land Use Committee voted 'Yes' to a slightly modified plan—it added morsels of affordable housing and a few more acres of park—and Councilman Yassky reversed himself. 'It's transformative,' he said. This was true, in one sense: Williamsburg would be transformed. The plan with its waterfront 'esplanade,' Yassky crowed, added 'yet another publicly accessible jewel to New York City's waterfront.' Like most jewels, this one would rest inside a glass case. The Williamsburg waterfront went from being one of the most open places in Brooklyn to one of the most restricted.

When the final vote went through, Teddy's threw a party with Yassky as the guest of honor. The owner of Teddy's was on the board of NAG, Neighbors Allied for Good Growth. NAG had started as 'Neighbors Against Garbage' to oppose the building of a waste transfer station on Kent. Good growth meant different things to different people. Thirty thousand more customers on the Northside wouldn't hurt Teddy's bottom line.

Architecture is where money gets naked. Every trust-fund kid can go to the same dive bars as you. He can wear the same thrift-store fashions, use the same slang, listen to the same bands. He can talk about the novel he's working on or the canvas he just stretched. Get to be friends and you'll eventually figure it out—he'll mention the two months in New Zealand or the family place in Truro, and there won't be much groaning about a day job. Walk into his home, though, and you'll know right away. A two-thousand-square-foot loft with an enormous flat screen, a darkroom, a granite fireplace, mahogany paneling and a cast-iron spiral staircase.

No gig riding a truck as an art handler is going to pay for that. Meet the competition, young bohemian.

When Congress opened the Indian Territories north of Texas in 1889, fifty thousand settlers crossed the border in a day. Today we call that place 'Oklahoma,' which means 'red people' in Choctaw. In the case of Williamsburg, the land grabbers weren't Civil War vets, freedmen and Scotch-Irish southerners with surnames like Allison, McLaughlin and McCabe; they were corporations—LeFrak, Key and Select. The stampede favored the strong, although strength in the case of the Greenpoint-Williamsburg land rush meant money and lawyers rather than Winchesters and Conestogas. In both cases, natives and old-timers like me scratched our heads as the future trampled us.

I thought that dot-com had taught me about the power of money. The real estate boom showed me that I didn't know anything about money. I didn't know that the Wall Street wizards could perform acts of prestidigitation that made the stunts of the Bindlestiff Family Cirkus seem infantile. For finance magicians, the Williamsburg-Greenpoint rezoning was only a card trick, a warm-up in a world tour that swept six continents. Dot-com put businesses on Bedford and young, well-educated people into long-empty buildings. The real estate boom demolished entire blocks and erected condo towers in their places.

When the dot-com bubble burst I thought that the neighborhood would calm down. That people had learned their lessons, that my Williamsburg would have more time. I was wrong, again. The real estate boom dwarfed the dot-com boom. Real estate money took the waterfront and reshaped it, adding new piers, marinas and seawalls. Gangs of laborers dug pits and erected scaffolding, the huge cranes turning residents into dumbstruck spectators at the creation of a new city. The dot-com boom made history run faster; the real estate boom erased history. If you came to the Northside for the first time in 2008 it was impossible to imagine what it had looked like five years earlier. I wasn't even sure myself. I'd walk to the waterfront and get lost, see a rubble heap covering a city block and try to picture the warehouse that had stood there for a hundred years. My memory was being erased. Rush hour on the subway platform had already become Japanese in its compression, and tens of thousands of new bodies were about to be dumped on the concrete that was left.

How to Become a Rock Star

I heard Gerard before I saw him. As I waited on the subway platform, a flurry of notes from a classical guitar floated past, knitting air. The Bedford L drew buskers, often of high quality; you have to practice somewhere, and spare change comes in handy. I got a picture of the new musician over the weeks: late twenties, Carhartt jacket, brambled dreads rising from his scalp. I put a few dollars in his case when I was flush: he could *play*, the bills received with a faint nod. He bent over his Del Pilar guitar with a pained expression and I'd drift on melodic lines until the train came. You don't often see black hobos playing classical guitar—unless you're in New York. Sometimes he'd accompany a singer, a short white girl with a Dennis-the-Menace haircut who sounded like Janis Joplin before the whiskey.

The Bedford Street L station had an embarrassment of platform talent. Another guitarist, Howard Fishman, had a repertoire of early-twentieth-century pop tunes and dressed like a refugee from the *Dust Bowl Ballads*. An inebriated Pole weaved along the platform with an accordion; he played Polish weddings, and I'd see him servicing the receptions in McCarren Park on the weekends, as melancholy and drunk with his squeezebox in sunlight as he was underground.

Paychecks, not music, brought Gerard to Williamsburg. Like a lot of art-school guys who were good with their hands, Gerard had ended up in the building trades, in his case, metal work. His employer's shop was in the neighborhood and nine to five on the Northside led him to the subway.

Gerard had gone straight from high school in Plainview, Long Island, to a summer art intensive at the Pratt Institute in Clinton Hill. His focus was visual arts—graphic design, painting, printmaking. What made Gerard different from other anguished teen devotees of Morrissey was his West Indian background and the fact that he'd started taking classical guitar lessons at age three. Growing up in the brain death of the suburbs is rough on any sensitive soul, but it was even harder for a black kid in a white town. Gerard wouldn't fake his way as a hip-hop stud—he dug Neil Young—any more than he would join the suburban jock world of letter jackets and beer pong. He had the instincts and in Brooklyn he would find style.

Pratt led Gerard to the oxymoronic Fashion Institute of Technology and from there he went to the SUNY art school, Purchase. Although he was at Purchase for fine art and art history, Gerard played guitar more than he studied. Purchase is also where he met Malcolm, the singer with the bowl haircut. Even though she sang Gerard's songs, it was Malcolm that the music scouts slipped a business card when they heard her remarkable voice. After a few years on the welding job and the grind of busking, Gerard ended up pouring

coffee at the Verb. We talked shit for months before I realized that the hyper guy making chai lattes was the same
musician I'd seen in the subway: he'd whacked the dreads,
and in his Carhartt jacket and short Afro, he looked more
longshoreman than busker. It was a hard time for him; you
couldn't make a living playing classical, especially if you
didn't have the degrees, and immigrant parents want their
kids to get real jobs.

The metalworker/barista/art-school dropout was one of
the most animated men I've ever met, like Road Runner on
Ritalin. Look up for a second while he was behind the counter and he'd notice your glance. When we talked his eyes always scanned: the counter, the room, the street through the
Verb picture windows. His body quivered, frame wavering
like he was made from some unstable element, the same
frazzled look Snoopy took on when Charles Schulz kept
drawing the strip after he got Parkinson's. The only time the
trembling stopped was when Gerard leaned over his guitar.

The Verb scene was different from the L's of a few years
earlier. The Verb was the center of a community but not one
based in the neighborhood—the Verb fellowship stretched
across the boroughs. People made pilgrimages to drink
smooth Verb iced coffee and ask the barista what cool CD
was playing. I understood the impulse: in 1992, I took the A
train from 168th Street to West Fourth every weekend and
hiked across town to Café Limbo on Avenue A. I made the
trip because I wanted to feel at home. Verb denizens were
better off than the old Williamsburg crowd—better clothes,
better style, better manners. I hadn't seen models sipping
lattes at the L (Magda didn't quite count).

Put 'musician' on your Verb application and you got
hired. Every barista was in a band, the manager too, a la-

conic lesbian who dressed like Gene Vincent. None of the Verb baristas lived on the Northside—they couldn't afford to. For them the Northside wasn't home: it was an audition, ground zero for a career launch. Musicians need clubs, audiences, a vibe; when I first moved to Williamsburg it lacked such things. Of course, musicians had lived in Williamsburg from the beginning and played lofts there, but when they had a real show they took their instruments and got on the subway or into a van and went to Brownies and CBGB. Later, building code–challenged clubs like Rubulad, Llano Estacado and Mighty Robot dodged fire marshals to showcase bands, but you still felt like you were at a loft party.

The Bindlestiff shows at Gargoyle and the Brewery didn't have bands. That was a good thing. Bands dominate celebration: they shut you out as a comrade and turn you into a spectator. Every rock band has a fascist soul, a fascist who wants you to lick his boots as he crushes you and sixty thousand other worshippers in an outdoor stadium. Fascism explains why every hit song is an anthem—exultation comes from spectacle and volume, a Nuremberg rally with the ideology extracted so it can sell. 'Message, what message?' the rock Nazi says. '*I* am the message.' Even the explicitly anti-anthem lyric in a song like 'Nevermind' is swept away by 4/4 guitar crash and a catchy melody.

By 2003, the Williamsburg music scene was a national draw. Stinger Club and Trash Bar opened on Grand and a thicket of clubs ran down North Sixth to the water—Galapagos, Zablozki's, the cleverly named Northsix, along with half a dozen others between the bridge and McCarren Park. In a new-order city where you had to make it young or not make it at all, the rock band was the perfect model. In the eighties, the New York scene had been eclipsed by the rise of regional centers—in the Twin Cities, Seattle, Austin—but Williamsburg became the hub of a New York renaissance with the Strokes (sort of), Yeah Yeah Yeahs, Interpol, Animal Collective, Fischerspooner. Word had it that electro-clash was born in a Kokie's booth. Even if those bands weren't officially from Williamsburg, the band members spent a lot of time at the Verb, on both sides of the counter.

I'd be un-American if I said that rock music and rock shows didn't matter to me. I'd also be lying. My first concert was at age thirteen at the Providence Civic Center, a triple bill of the Joe Perry Project (Aerosmith was on heroin hiatus), Foghat and Blue Öyster Cult. At the concert, Tara Goldberg gave me my first slurp on a joint. (Then she complained that I 'nigger-lipped' it. I hadn't even puffed on a cigarette before.) Although Taras D-cups allowed her to date college boys, she thought I was cute. Cuteness didn't get me kissed—I was too weird—but the concert was an introduction to a lawless adult universe. Over the next decade I trekked to a lot of shows in a lot of places, but I soon learned that clubs were better than stadiums and that music sounded better if you knew the people onstage.

I have clearer memories of a friend's band playing sloppy REM-ish tunes in a basement on Dexter Avenue than I do of a Neil Young solo show at the Civic Center the same year. I knew those other Providence kids: I partied with them, argued with them, slept on their stained couches when I was fighting with my father. A college friend had connections in the music industry and he got us VIP room passes at the Ritz on East Eleventh Street. Doing lines in the Ritz bathroom right after Hillel Slovak came out wiping his nose was a thrill at twenty, but it wasn't as good as slam-dancing to Saccharine Trust at the Living Room because Joe Baiza came over to my apartment afterward and—when he realized my roommate wasn't going to fuck him—talked to me about how Miles Davis influenced his solos. The media blares away about the lives of actors, divas, guitarists and athletes, trying to convince us that we're all in high school together.

In Williamsburg all those years later, music still mattered to me. At the Verb the baristas/rock-stars-in-waiting would tell me that their bandmates were lazy, or on drugs, or had gotten their girlfriends pregnant, turned off their cell phones and moved back to Arkansas. They talked about how they wanted their records to sound, how they'd go back to school when they couldn't bear being broke anymore. I'd troop to the Tuesday night showcase at Rock Star Bar on Kent and pay the five-dollar cover because a friend was playing and we could talk about it the next day at the Verb. Mostly I was a spectator nodding my head and looking at the clock. But then came the other times . . . when a Verb regular who looked like she got dressed in the dark channeled a demon and had the entire crowd at Zebulon dancing between the tables; or when the shabby barista whose constant intake of coffee and cocaine made it impossible for him to keep his eyes open managed, after a year of big talk, to astonish Union Pool with Beatlesque harmonies.

I was surprised to hear that Gerard had joined TV On The Radio. TVOTR had taken an unusual path to success: they didn't exist on Monday and by Wednesday they had a hit; on the weekend, David Bowie showed up for a guest vocal. Napoleon told me that Tunde Adebimpe and Dave Sitek, the founding members, first discussed starting a band when they were hanging out in his apartment. The two men were roommates, or neighbors, something like that, in a building on Havemeyer. Sitek was a producer, and after he recorded the Yeah Yeah Yeahs's *Fever to Tell*, he had leverage. The duo got signed by Touch and Go even though no one on the label had seen them perform, and soon they had a campus hit under the name TV On The Radio. It was at that point that they brought in Kyp Malone.

Yet another Verb barista, Kyp was the most popular man on the Northside. We called him the mayor of Williamsburg. Every hipster doll in Williamsburg seemed to want nothing more from life than a hug from Daddy Malone—hug posses would clog the Verb floor as women waited for their embrace. At Radio Free Williamsburg, upstairs from Gargoyle, I'd seen Kyp play a kind of avant-jazz noise rock far from the indie pop of TVOTR. The choice of Kyp for the band had as much to do with his local celebrity as his chops—people went to see Kyp to see Kyp—but the band was more concept than touring unit. Sitek's idea for performances was to open a gold suitcase onstage and draw out his pedals and sequencers. This worked so well that some of the first TVOTR shows ended up being a cappella.

Like me, Tunde had heard Gerard busking at the Bedford station and been blown away by his chops. The need for more talent brought Gerard into the band. It didn't hurt *at all* that, like the drummer and Kyp, he was black. Of course, Gerard took the gig; it was an offer a starving artist couldn't refuse.

Williamsburg was diverse—you had a hundred different kinds of crazy to pick from—but it was pretty damn white. A couple of Asians, a few Hispanics, even fewer African Americans. Black people didn't join bohemia in numbers; there were fewer of them in the middle classes and more pressure on the artistic souls to become professionals. Pop music requires a look—David Bowie the extraterrestrial, Stevie Nicks the hippie witch. TVOTR had a look to win. The Verb joke was that when TVOTR went on tour, it cut the black population of the neighborhood in half.

The band got famous almost before we knew it existed. A friend who worked at Main Drag Music couldn't believe the mob that showed up at the release party for *Desperate Youth, Blood Thirsty Babes*. 'The show sold out,' he says. 'And I was shocked that I didn't recognize anyone there. Not one person. They didn't live in Williamsburg. TVOTR didn't build themselves up locally like Grizzly Bear and Interpol. It was the first show in Williamsburg where I didn't at least recognize people in the crowd.' It's always disconcerting when your friends become celebrities. The guys I knew best in the band, Gerard and Kyp, didn't change for the worse. Kyp just had to hug even more people when he walked down Bedford.

In TVOTR Gerard was assigned to the bass, an instrument he didn't know, but then the drummer, Jaleel Bunton, another guitarist, had never played drums before, either. To their credit, Sitek and Adebimpe divided all TVOTR income equally with the rest of the band. For Gerard, it was the rock-and-roll dream come true—one day he was pouring coffee at the Verb and the next he was doing shed tours and gracing the covers of music magazines. His loyalty to a neighborhood he'd outgrown kept me interested in the band. When a Verb barista told me TVOTR was playing a 'secret' show at Trash Bar, Nadia and I ran down to Grand and pushed into the crowd. The energy was high, the room was shaking. Through the crush I could make them out onstage, for the time being still in the same room as us.

Success didn't make Gerard complacent; if anything, he got more intense. His partner, Jessica, had a child soon after he joined the band, and that tied him more closely to TVOTR; dads can't turn down paychecks. So Gerard went out and he toured. In the band, he played disciplinarian—making sure that everyone stuck to the rehearsal schedule until the live shows got tight. When he walked into the Verb during a busy shift, he'd head behind the counter and start making drinks and handling the register for old times' sake. I'd see him driving around the neighborhood in the beat-up VW minibus TVOTR used to move equipment. When he was in town he'd complain about the hardships of the road. 'I'm so tired of guitars,' he said. 'If I have to see another guitar band I'll slit my wrists. Guitars should cost thirty thousand dollars. And amps should cost a quarter of a million.' That he was in a guitar band himself, well, that made the joke even funnier. Gerard always thought of himself as a guitarist, and having to play bass felt like trading in a Maserati for a station wagon.

When it came to writing and recording with TVOTR, Gerard stayed in the background. It wasn't that Gerard didn't feel grateful, it just wasn't his baby. Instead he took the free time he had to work on his own projects; at the Verb one afternoon he plugged me into his Sony Discman (no iPod, he was a Luddite) so I could hear a series of charming ukulele demos. From the road he'd call Jessica and talk excitedly about the museums and historic sites he'd visited. Gerard tried to use his new superpowers for good, introducing musicians he thought should work together, producing records, and composing the sound track for a film, *The Lottery*. He started a contest in which he gave his favorite musicians a short lyric and told them they had to make a song from it. One of the best lines, 'Baby, I dig your magic,' turned into a compilation record.

We all would have liked to have Gerard's celebrity problems, but he was moral in an old-fashioned way, the legacy maybe of West Indian roots. Morality compelled him to tip 40 percent when he ate out (and he ate out a lot). It explained why he volunteered as a welder on the 9/11 site. Gerard knew that TVOTR was a springboard to musical freedom; all he needed was patience, persistence and time. At thirty-five, time seemed to be the least of those concerns.

February 2007

At several points in late 2006, Nadia broke up with me, tired of waiting for that two-bedroom Williamsburg apartment. On her third try the breakup took. Six years is a long time to be with someone, and breaking up seemed to take ten times as long. At night I'd sit in my apartment until I started gasping like a pigeon in Robert Boyle's air pump. Of course, I didn't have health insurance, so there was no doctor to tell me about depression and anxiety attacks and soothe me with Xanax. I had to get out but I wasn't running to parties anymore; I just needed to breathe. There had to be more air outside. Downstairs the miserable Goth runt had been replaced by an Iraq vet who painted and wrote poetry. He was an upgrade, but the bakery doors still slammed at three a.m. and Polish bakers still smoked and bellowed under my bedroom windows. The yard was too small and I kept going.

Williamsburg had always been a good place for a long walk. Movement makes you feel cleaner. I'd walked away from teen misery on the historic streets of the East Side of Providence. Sprinklers hissed and chucked over big green lawns and Victorian houses soothed the eye. The Providence neighborhoods didn't belong to me but at night they didn't belong to anybody else, either. I didn't mind empty streets—other people were the problem. Other people put you on guard and you shrank into your shell. In the dark I could be anonymous.

Twenty-five years later I had a few advantages over teenage Robert Anasi. More money, for one, and a driver's license that said I was old enough. I could go into a restaurant and have a late dinner. I could sail into a bar for a quick shot. My shell was hard and polished. You had to stand really close to see the cracks.

Out front, I'd turn right toward Berry to avoid the Bedford mob. Across the street over Planet Thailand rose the spindle of a 'finger' building. It had been giving us the finger for four years. 'Finger building' was a term applied to those new buildings on small lots that jumped hundreds of feet over neighboring roofs. Even though the Greenpoint-Williamsburg Plan restricted heights away from the waterfront, developers ranked above civil servants on the Bloomberg food chain and generally ate what they wanted. A good three handfuls of fingers had been injected into Williamsburg during the land rush. Plastic sheeted the sixteen-story skeleton because hubris over zoning had caught it in the quicksand of the courts. The finger quivered in its plastic, constrained from fructifying the clouds.

Catty-corner from Teddy's on Berry was the Brooklyn Ale House. When it opened in late 1997, the owner described the bar as 'upscale downtown without the attitude.' Translated from codespeak he meant that it resembled East Village saloons but with more people who paid for drinks with their own money. He wasn't far from right. With its pool table and groovy jukebox, the Ale House reminded me of Joe's Bar on East Sixth, my haven in the 1990s. The Ale House had more Poles and firefighters (from the 'People's Firehouse' on Wythe—closed by Bloomberg in 2003) than Joe's, and the girls had tattoos and pierced navels. Locals had dubbed it the 'Tail House,' a name any bar would wear with honor.

On the corner of North Ninth and Berry, another bar posed as a speakeasy. White paint bleared the plate-glass windows and a folding iron gate blocked the front door. Around the corner at the side door, a bouncer posed like he was waiting for a password or secret handshake (he just wanted to see your ID). In underlit rooms you crossed worn tile and sat at tables with scarred marble tops. Bottles of absinthe lined the shelves. 'Something not quite legal is going on in here,' the bar whispered. 'Don't you want to be part of it?'

I walked north on Berry past condos that had morphed from warehouse rows. One of the former warehouses had been faced in faux white granite. When a car rolled to the entrance, a Buckingham Palace guard dashed out to open the door. I turned the corner of North Twelfth and passed the Turkey's Nest. I remembered a night I'd gone there with Rebecca, my Trotskyist-cum-contractor friend Ben, and some of the crew. In a city where all waiters are actors, all carpenters are artists. Ben had an army of architects and painters sawing boards and hauling rubble. That night we also had Willem Dafoe's understudy with us. Rebecca called him James Taylor because he dressed like a hippie and had reached the venerable age of thirty-nine. Being Dafoe's under-study made him an arrogant prick, and disappointment made him an even bigger prick: he wasn't Willem Dafoe and he had to huff paint fumes and sawdust to pay bills.

I remember the night in high-def: we were celebrating

the end of a big project, we were drunk, and we shoved each other into every snowbank along the way. All the guys were hitting on Rebecca because she was the only girl and because she was beautiful.

The Turkey's Nest was still a dive bar. Hasidic pool sharks still came in to hustle, cues in leather cases, sidelocks dangling as they leaned over for shots. Italian and Puerto Rican guys still played league softball on the concrete field across the street and stood in front of the bar in their uniforms after games, bellowing and smoking. A three-hundred-pound guido still peddled bad coke next to the video games. Frank Versace had introduced me to the connect. The Nest had been on Frank's way home from the L and it would ambush him before he could get away. 'Just one drink, I'd tell myself,' Frank said. 'You know how that goes. Next thing, you're in bed with a woman who has parts where there aren't supposed to be parts.'

The girls I'd brought home had all the right parts in all the right places. I once saw a one-woman show in the theater above the KGB Bar in the East Village. From the moment the spotlight hit her faded jeans, a white hole high on one round thigh, I wanted to fuck her. This made sense: the whole point of the show was to make you want to fuck her. We didn't talk that night but a mutual friend brought her to a Williamsburg party and she came back to 147. We had sex on the foldout couch because our friend, Helena, was having sex in my bed with a Polish guy she'd picked up at the Tail House. In earliest morning Helena walked into the living room wearing nothing but my Everlast groin protector and a pair of boxing gloves. She asked us if we wanted to share. I said no. I didn't want to share. (Helena had published a successful first novel but then she got sick. On a trip to the bodega for milk, a vein in her skull ruptured and she died before her forty-first birthday, leaving thousands of draft pages of the second novel.) There was the German model who talked to me at the Verb because I was reading Hegel's *Phenomenology of Spirit* (not a conversation that happens every day). She lived on the corner of Berry and North Sixth and I'd read poetry to her because she liked the burble of my English. Through her two high grilled windows we'd listen to the workers in the meat-processing plant next door toss sacks of blood and offal. Later we'd hear the partyers outside Sweetwater growing louder into two a.m. and then, after three, the sound falling away. One afternoon, I walked in and she slid her hand down her jeans and pushed her fingers into my mouth. 'See how wet you make me?' she said. There was a filmmaker who didn't like her curves because it drew the wrong demographic. 'Hipster guys like skeletons,' she said. 'They think I'm a sumo wrestler. I only get hit on by Spanish guys.' I must have Spanish blood because I watched her in my shower and thought about how much better she looked without her clothes. There were others too—the girl with the animal green eyes who took off her clothes before we even kissed, got into my bed and then vomited into a bowl. The journalist who came over disguised in a black wig and said, 'What does a girl have to do to get fucked in the ass around here?' Even though I felt alone a lot of the time, I wasn't always. Nothing was better than that moment when I knew it would happen: at the party when the actress—her voice the perfect world-weary New York cigarette rasp—and I touched and then pressed together, back-to-back, pressing down our arms all the way down to our hands, and my entire body ached; at the Blue Lounge with the model, all six-foot-one of her, tall and strong, and

209   2004-2008

she covertly pressed her leg against mine while the three guys with us looked at her like she was a cross between the Louvre and a breakfast burrito. When that moment came those guys weren't competition anymore, just a nuisance we wanted to go away. Sex was the best drug of all. 'The moment of desire! The moment of desire!' Blake writes, exclamation points essential. Drugs make time meaningless and real passion is the best drug of all. But where drugs make you hate the morning after, passion opens a place where time can be embraced. I'd shared my flimsy bed with amazing women and the best times it felt like it had never happened before and that it would go on forever. It never did.

When you're sleeping alone, memory doesn't keep you warm. When I was twenty-six, I had an affair with a photographer who just happened to look like a brunette Botticelli Venus. In bed one morning she cautioned me against sleeping with anyone over forty. 'Don't do it,' she said. 'Something happens to their skin.' She shuddered. The fact that she'd had sex with someone so ancient added to her mystery but it didn't seem like something I'd ever have to worry about. Fourteen years later, I was older than James Taylor when Rebecca mocked his denim jacket. My skin still looked okay but that wasn't the only place age showed.

I crossed Bedford into McCarren Park. Across the field, a squad car monitored the entrance, headlights furrowing grass. I skirted the lights and went north past the baseball diamonds with their batting cages and base paths. Warm weekends turned the park into a hipster beach, blankets and pale bodies slathered on every patch of ground. Months had passed since the last warm day, but the darkest park corners held limp bodies, Rip van Winkles waiting for spring. Next to the fence, four men with metal T's and caveman beards sprawled in a mess of paper-wrapped bottles, their feet touching, heads the points of a satanic compass. Under a streetlamp at the side of the path a Polish man lay facedown, bald patch glowing red. A few yards away, another Pole was faceup, his cheeks the same angry color. On a bench under a broken streetlamp I noticed a curving black line and thought, 'Woman's hip.' The curled form wore capri pants and a black sweater. Closer, I noticed her ghostly face. It was the madwoman of Bedford Avenue. Earlier that week she'd stopped me in front of the Salvation Army storefront. 'The Hasids are after me,' she said, clinging to my arm. 'They said they were going to take me out. You should be concerned. The way they take somebody out is by taking somebody else out, and then blaming it on you. They want to sacrifice me. It's because my family was poor.'

I was fertile ground for sidewalk prophecy. Semi-domestic life—Nadia had cats, we watched *The Daily Show*—had given me security but I wouldn't leave the Northside, so I'd been left. I looked up, alone again, and Williamsburg wasn't the same. Kokie's was gone. The L Café was gone. There weren't many scuffling artists. There wasn't as much space.

I'd never had a plan for life; I just wanted smart people to read me and fall in love. All the smart people. Everywhere. With my first book the future had seemed clear. Old Roger Straus came out of his office and patted me on the back and it felt like I'd gotten the medal of honor from Abraham Lincoln. But Roger had died and—true story—the guy reviewing my book for *The New York Times*, another very old man, dropped dead with my rave review in his typewriter. The review never ran. I didn't have a backup plan. I was as broke at forty as I'd been at thirty but Campbell's soup didn't go down so easily. It cost more too.

I crossed Driggs to the soccer field where I'd played hundreds of pickup games. For most of those games we scrambled over a mess of dirt and rock. Dust clouds browned the air and dust veneered our clothes and skin. After every tackle we stood up bloody and no detergent could remove the stains. The players were mostly Latinos with a few Poles and Americans and Euro travelers in the mix. Despite the excess of testosterone and machismo, there weren't many fights, just a lot of bitching over bad passes and fouls. Then the city put down a beautiful crumb-rubber infill surface and erected stadium lights. The night before the official opening we jumped the fences and played for hours. The ball slid across the turf like an icicle in zero g. 'Check out those lights!' we said. 'This is so smooth! Now you'll see my skills! No more bruises! I'm going to be out here six days a week!' Within months, league games filled the calendar, teams with permits coming in from across the borough. It was a microcosm of the changed neighborhood: when you have something good, everyone wants it, and everyone else is better organized than you. So we migrated across the street, except those fields had been claimed for baseball and softball and something called 'hipster kickball.' Hipster kickball rules required that participants lack all athletic talent. The rules also called for female participants to dress like strippers in vintage gym shorts or poodle skirts three sizes too tight and knee-highs over shapely calves. (Hipster girls were always in better shape than hipster boys.) As we tried to get our soccer game going in deepest center field, the Latin guys would ogle the hipster girls as if woman had just been invented, right there on the Northside. No Michoacán *muchachas* dressed like that for the *zocalo*.

At night the pitch was dark but east across Bayard twin

searchlights probed the sky. The Semer Sleep Mattress factory where Chris Mis had smoked bowls while admiring the Manhattan backdrop had been reincarnated as high-end condos. A banner drooping on the glass façade proclaimed 'Grand Opening' and searchlights wheeled. The apartments weren't built out yet—a construction elevator crawled up the building side like a metal tick on a robot dog—but a flyer someone had stuck in my hand at the subway entrance said that model units were open for viewing. From the field, I could see stick figures wandering through the models, backlit by fluorescents blazing on every floor. 'Williamsburg is just a big construction site,' Nadia had said on her last visit. She was right; you felt like you should put on a hard hat every time you left the house. Four other condo projects were going up on the same block and three more to the north on Manhattan and Driggs.

On the other side of the BQE, new bars and restaurants spread down Union and Lorimer, in place to service the condos rising around them. I wasn't ready to crawl back under my bell jar, so I decided to brave the Bedford crowds and go to the waterfront. The week before, I'd left my front door open and stepped into a film set—production gnomes had set it up overnight and put buffet tables at the foot of my staircase. When no one was looking, I swiped a Danish, small tithe for the fact that over the following three days I had to tell the fat men with walkie-talkies that yes, actually, I lived on the street. The film shoot wasn't unusual—on the Northside they ran continuously. My guess was that lazy location scouts looked out from the windows of their $4,000 a month one-bedrooms and said, 'Uh, why don't we just shoot here.' On the Bedford corner tourists rubbernecked. 'Did you see Alec Baldwin?' a girl said, breathless.

My landlady lived between North Eleventh and Twelfth, a block down from a paint factory that had been demolished seven years earlier. Nothing had gone up on the site, although for a while a sign on the fence had proclaimed an imminent Starbucks. Behind the fence, a few dismal weeds pushed through the field of concrete and splintered brick. Rumor had it that the ground was so polluted no developer would take on the cleanup costs and that strong winds dispersed a toxic cloud.

I assumed I paid my rent in cash because my landlady didn't carry insurance on my building and because she wanted to hide the income. She received me like I was a peasant in the manor house and counted out bills on the kitchen table like a cardsharp (she'd been a bookkeeper in Poland) as she shared the latest gossip and discussed her medical issues in relentless detail.

I am having problems with my back, she'd told me on my last visit.

Yes, she said. Even when I am lying down, it hurts. I think I need to have more sex.

Sex?

Sex helps, she said. But my boyfriend not gives me enough.

She cackled, unconcerned that the boyfriend, a stout Polish building super, was parked in front of her television with her demented Chihuahua.

Maybe he needs Viagra, I said.

How much this cost? she said.

I don't know, I said.

Can you get this for me?

I told her I'd look into it. The conversation somehow moved on to the fact that I was circumcised. At this information, Henryka brightened.

Then you are Jew! she said.

Her kitchen and living room were straight immigrant kitsch—the family photos in heavy frames, the plastic-covered couch, the big-screen TV always droning. Her garden was beautiful, though, a rain forest in the urban jungle. She led me out to the last flowers of the season. More than the flowers and the rosebushes and the deep-green lawn, the sound struck me, a shrill and manic piping. Her yard was backed by a brick wall over forty feet high. Throughout Brooklyn old residential rows had those walls, with narrow iron ladders and laundry lines strung from rungs to windows. Ivy enveloped the wall and the leaves pulsed although there was no breeze. The sound came from inside the ivy: hundreds of birds—sparrows, pigeons, starlings, finches—clinging to branches and shrieking and launching as other birds darted in. Birds also filled the one large tree in the yard, bustling on the limbs.

They are very upset, Henryka said.

She told me that the warehouses on the other side of the wall had been knocked down and condos were going up in their place. For the first time I noticed the head of a crane jutting above the wall. She told me that demolition had already started.

They're knocking down the wall? I said. But it's beautiful. You should take them to court.

I can do nothing, she said. It belong to them.

Communist Poland had made Henryka a realist. In the future, two-bedroom millionaires would stare into her garden from their balconies.

On any weekend without hail, flood or whiteout blizzard, Bedford was an all-hours lotus party, dying with a whimper in the backwash of Sunday morning, gutters mired with cigarette butts, broken glass and shredded paper, the last partyers drained by booze and drugs and sex making their walks of shame. In the day, the Northside was 'Baby-burg.' Kelly had married an architect and they lived in a loft building on the Southside with their daughter. From my table at the Verb I'd see her pushing a baby carriage and we'd talk outside. We'd kept a writers' group going for almost a year but babies get in the way of literature. Once on Bedford, I'd seen Rebecca behind a baby carriage but when she noticed me, she turned and crossed the street.

At night the Northside was 'Bedford Campus' and I jostled along with the student body. The line for Anna Maria, the pizza place across from the Charleston, spilled out the door. When it first opened, old Benny wouldn't let you into the Charleston if you bought Anna Maria's pizza instead of his—but he and Agnes sold the bar and vanished into oldest age. A phalanx of cops held the subway corner, the 24th Foot at Rorke's Drift braced for the next wave of Zulus. Two men in blazers waited at the light and the taller tried to define the phenomenon: 'It's like SoHo eight years ago,' he said.

The L To-Go store was now Fornino, a gourmet pizzeria with a woodburning stove, and the café was Bagelsmith, one of four bagel stores on Bedford. The ghost of Frank the Bum didn't wander into Fornino and insult me as I sat over a twenty-dollar wood-cooked pie topped with organic arugula from the owner's greenhouse. What I felt was more disorienting: all the landmarks had changed and I didn't have anything to hold on to. It wasn't like I'd spent twenty years in prison or Antarctica and grown so ugly that old friends said, 'Who the hell are you?' I was a senior citizen at a scene from my childhood telling the people who lived in my old house, 'We used to have a peach tree in the backyard.'

The Williamsburg I lived in was a time-lapse world, history on fast forward.

Across Bedford from the subway exit, vendors manned a line of tables. In the fall I'd seen Frank there behind a table of his own. After the L debacle, we'd lost touch. His table was covered with T-shirts he silkscreened—fanged plants and menacing anthropomorphic landscapes. He'd changed: shoulders muscled, his head no longer skewing right. Frank told me that yoga and kung fu had saved his life. All the partying had been a form of self-medication. 'I was getting energy from the earth meridian and it was adding to the already messed-up energy in my body,' he said. He told me that a tangled chi flow had misaligned his nerves and muscles and sent him spiraling into chaos. Now the energy flows were ordered and he shared his apartment with a pregnant girlfriend. The next time I heard from him had been the previous week, when he invited me over to meet his son. To see Frank cradling a child as infant fingers plucked his collar was a blissful shock.

In front of one of the three East Asian restaurants between North Fifth and Sixth, a blond skater kid slumped over his Vans and a spreading red pool. 'Blood,' I thought, but no one reacted to his violent death. Moving closer, I noticed chunks in the red fluid. The kid had emptied himself of dinner and an energy drink mixed with booze. A friend with an unfortunate beard stood next to him, shuffling feet and looking down, loyalty fraying. The sick boy slumped against the restaurant's French doors but couples inside kept putting forks into faces. It didn't have anything to do with them.

I'd run into Marcin with his daughter in front of the same restaurant a few days earlier. She was an adorable child, with his dark Gypsy eyes and floss-silk hair. In her father's face, the eyes were bagged and deeply circled. His expensive chinos would have billowed on the old Marcin but prosperity had inflated him. As the girl swung from her father's hand, Marcin told me stories that were years away from her comprehension. Judith was deep into heroin again. She was so out of control, Marcin said, that he didn't want to leave the child alone with her. I'd heard from a mutual friend that Marcin was her husband's pot dealer and that, in a panic the month before, Marcin had asked her to take custody of their daughter. When I mentioned our friend, Marcin gave his conspiratorial laugh and said, 'I bet you heard very good stories from her.' As he left he said, 'Oh, Robert. Larry Clark is going to make a movie about me. About me and drugs.'

I reversed direction and turned west on North Seventh, passing an upscale Korean market where organic kale chips would set you back three dollars an ounce. Through a wall of windows I looked into the Planet Thailand compound. The restaurant had just closed for the night and on the flat-screen TV over the bar a pretty East Asian woman on a lawn chair was masturbating. Her scene was intercut with one of a man doing sit-ups beside a pool. No one was at the bar or down the gray length of restaurant. The small jolt bolstered my faith in Williamsburg. There was still a bit of sleaze left.

The waterfront had always been my refuge. When the state of New York bought the waterfront blocks from North Sixth through Eighth, we felt pretty good about it. The other option had been a 'waste transfer station.' Garbage trucks rolling through the neighborhood 24/7, diesel exhaust and more filth in a neighborhood of asthma and strange cancers. There was rejoicing: we stopped the garbagemen! We got our park! I went to the hearing at Van Arsdale High School, where the garbage company reps argued their case and we shouted them out of the room. It occurred to me that garbage would have kept the developers away, or as the distinguished sociologist Robert K. Merton frames it: 'Any intervention in a complex system may or may not have the intended result, but will inevitably create unanticipated and often undesirable outcomes.' Undesirable outcomes surrounded me: every month more of my waterfront disappeared.

Bodies blocked the intersection of North Sixth and Berry and cars horned frustration. North Sixth was for music and clubs and restaurants with fountains and plastic love-seat swings, plus an Urban Outfitters and an all-night diner, Anytime, that had made its owners wealthy by delivering booze and cigarettes right to your apartment. The meat-processing plant remained. They 'fabricated' veal and sold it wholesale. In the afternoon the fabricators grabbed lunch at a silver truck. They wore the white smocks of surgeons, those other craftsmen of death. Clumps of ice melted in the gutter and the sidewalk always smelled of corruption.

I moved down Berry through the crowd, away from the shouts and bass-thud that rattled suspensions like potholes. Just past North Sixth an eggplant purple Acura started following me, headlights prodding my back. I tensed, wondering if it was frat louts looking for a scrap.

Hey, someone shouted from the Acura. A woman's voice. I ignored her.

Hey! she said, louder.

I turned.

Are you going to your car? she said.

I didn't know what she was talking about. I didn't have a car.

Are you going to your car! she said, as patient as a nurse in the psych ward.

No, I said.

As the Ac pulled away I realized she was looking for a parking space. Friday night in Williamsburg had turned into Sunday at the mall.

Over the next two blocks, old warehouse dark still held sway. On the other side of the street a man was walking two large dogs. One of the dogs slipped the leash and bounded toward me. I staggered back into a fence from the impact of a hundred and fifty pounds of Rottweiler.

Whoa! the man shouted. Whoa! Whoa!

He crossed the street as the Rottweiler teethed my arm.

Napoleon, I said.

What's up? he said, smiling. Loosing the dog was his way of saying hello.

Napoleon always walked late, another Williamsburg vampire. As we talked, the dogs lunged at my legs, making it hard to follow the conversation. Napoleon just laughed at my discomfort. He'd survived the neighborhood transition unscathed. Real estate was his new trade. For the right commission, he'd connect you to that rent-stabilized apartment or a loft selling under market. His mother had bought her building and he rented an entire floor from her. For Napoleon this was good business but his hipster friends teased him about living with Mom.

I left Napoleon and his slobbering bullies and turned west on North Third past the bar formerly known as Kokie's Place. Where the Antique Lounge had failed, the Levee thrived. The Levee had hot-plate chili and two-dollar cans of Black Label. It had a pool table and video games. The Levee was 'indie': tattoos and old T-shirts, skateboards and hard rock (like, yes, Zep's 'When the Levee Breaks'). The

Levee called itself a neighborhood bar but its neighborhood didn't live anywhere nearby. The regulars worked on the Northside—waiters and baristas and bartenders who needed to unwind before the subway ride home. I saw some Verb rock-stars-in-training outside but I avoided eye contact and kept walking. I still needed to catch my breath.

After the rezoning rubber stamp, construction permits went flying out of the Department of Buildings. By 2005 there were 130 new projects in the works and more requests, hundreds more, had been filed with the local community board—including a couple of buildings with more than 200 units apiece. Bloomberg called this 'harnessing the private market.' Harnessing the private market was a lot like the kid who tried to corral the chariots of the sun. Nowhere had Williamsburg changed as much as the Northside blocks between Berry and the water. They looked like Dresden circa 1945. On Berry and North Fourth, a pit had opened and swallowed an entire city block. I peered into the hole through planks painted blue, looking down at the concrete foundation. On North Fifth and Wythe, a former warehouse had been scavenged to a set of rusted steel girders. All along Kent, old auto yards and garages were rubble heaps, cranes a hundred feet over my head pecking at the bones.

Winston Churchill gets credit for the phrase 'History is written by the victors.' I have to disagree. Plenty of losers write history—this book, for instance—but the winners build it. As I walked down Kent, I felt like a truck-stop whore on the run from the Mafia. The business model had changed and I'd outlived my usefulness.

Blockbuster among coming attractions was the Edge, between North Fourth and North Sixth Streets. On the waterfront side of Kent, banners on Cyclone fences told us what to expect: 'Rock Bands + Stone Countertops,' 'Swimming

Pool + Shooting Pool,' 'The Hippest Dress Code + The Coolest Zip Code.' I wasn't sure how to respond: laughter, tears, projectile vomiting? At the Edge authenticity would be as accessible as the 'healing' whirlpool and salsa lessons downstairs. Three quarters of a million dollars would buy you one bedroom and proximity to cool.

In 2003, Robert Lanham, who lived around the corner from me, published *The Hipster Handbook* (9/11 had delayed it for a year). The book provided a mocking take on the subculture with entries like 'UTF (Unemployed Trust-Funder)': 'Hipsters who have the benefit of a wealthy family and are thus unencumbered by the distraction of a "straight" job.' Lanham even manufactured a vocabulary of hipster slang: cronkite, bleeker, bipster, boggle, bronson, deck. When I first looked at his glossary, it took me a blink to get the joke. No one I knew said 'deck,' maybe I wasn't cool anymore. Lanham captured the contradictions of the hipster pose: 'You enjoy complaining about gentrification even though you are responsible for it yourself.' His wry take on comfortable bohemians added to the hipster's ubiquity—by 2008, hipsters starred in ads for every compact car, new cologne and fast-food franchise trying to go upmarket.

The rise of the hipster brought reaction. 'All my students despise those hipster types,' a history professor at Boston College told me. The fact that the ad campaigns focused on male hipsters made them even more suspect—there was something very queer about men openly caring about the way they looked. We'd become the preppies of the new millennium, our lives a national joke.

And yet . . .

Despite their disdain for all those left-leaning, SUV-hating dudes in skinny jeans, Americans kept coming to

Williamsburg. They kept coming even though the neighborhood had become a parody of itself, a bohemian theme park. On a continent that had been straitjacketed into more of the same, Bedford Avenue tourists had left Bennigan's and the South Coast Plaza mall in search of something different. What they had wasn't good enough. There was some hope in that.

A bar that catered to the metal crowd, Duff's, had opened on the corner of North Third and Kent. At two a.m. metal nation was out in force, all black T-shirts and black leather and clouds of smoke over the winter-hardened street. Maybe Motörhead was in town. With the hearse parked in front and the shrunken heads on the walls, Duff's fit right in with Kent Street's industrial grunge. I didn't think many Edge folk would make Duff's their watering hole.

There was only one place I could still reach the water, one narrow passageway to the old world. It wasn't at 'our' park, the one we wrested away from the garbagemen, that stretch between North Ninth and North Sixth where I had roamed the marsh and skulked in abandoned buildings. Those buildings had been flattened, their rubble carted away. It was now East River State Park, with Ranger Rick in a green uniform. An iron fence painted black surrounded acres of lawn. Yoga moms pushed strollers, the rangers kicked you out at dusk and you couldn't ignore the curfew, not without going directly to jail. You couldn't jump the fence and hide from surveillance cameras, either: there was nowhere to hide—no tall stands of cordgrass, no abandoned buildings, no thorny bushes. It was just a park, green and sterile, with one species of plant—Kentucky bluegrass—and one species of bird—the pigeon—where the marsh had supported hundreds of both. A park surrounded by a big iron fence with spear-point posts. Anyway, you wouldn't want to go there after dark. There was nothing to stumble into, no piers, no danger, no mystery.

The last span of open waterfront stretched between Grand and North Third. On one side was Grand Ferry Park with its ferry memorial. On the North Third end was the huge Austin, Nichols warehouse that had been artists' lofts. A developer had seized the building and ejected the artists. In the before time, the waterfront always had fences but the holes had stayed open. New York City didn't care about a few holes. The Edge had added fences of its own, and any hole was patched the next morning. The Edge had security guards. The Edge had a maintenance budget. When the project manager picked up the phone, the NYPD took his calls. I'd crawled into the site a few times but a security guard had tracked me with a flashlight and I'd fallen waist-deep into slurry trying to escape.

Three enormous fuel storage tanks rose between the Edge and Grand Street Park. It was the last major industrial site on the Northside waterfront but New England Petroleum seemed to be losing its grip—debris piled against the tanks, and the fences were slashed. Once through the fence, you could climb ladders or staircases all the way up the tanks. You had to be careful, because it seemed like a squad car was always cruising down Kent. I had a hard time understanding why: fewer than a hundred people lived nearby. So I'd crouch behind a wall while the cruisers rolled, then hurry up the stairs to the maze of pipes and ducts and platforms. I'd brought Nadia there the year before. She'd fallen in love with the space too and shot a series of videos with parkour *traceurs* running and tumbling through the obstacles, their bodies staying in the air so long they made gravity seem optional.

If you climbed down the tanks on the waterfront side, you could wander along a series of floating bridges and piers. In those unhappy months, I'd spent hours watching Manhattan. The tide rocked the bridges under my shoes. 'Here it is,' I would tell myself. 'I can't be sad when I have this.' The black surface of the river rippled like mercury and a shore breeze stirred my hair.

That fall I'd sold a book proposal that I'd been shopping for two years. The slim advance allowed me to scrape by on freelance work: an occasional article, some copyediting gigs, a stint teaching ESL at a tourist school. When I taught ESL in my twenties, I loved it. I mean, James Joyce taught ESL. In San Francisco, my students were Chinese refugees who'd immigrated after Tiananmen Square. Most had been successful artists in China—a well-known novelist, a first violin in the Shanghai Symphony Orchestra, a painter whose blend of traditional landscapes and European Modernism landed him a cozy university post. In the United States, the artist worked in a glove factory and the violinist sold popcorn on Fisherman's Wharf (where he was attacked by a gang and beaten into a coma). The only reason they were at the school was to avoid deportation. I couldn't understand why they'd left comfortable lives to struggle in America. They smiled and murmured when I asked, too polite to make the earnest young teacher look stupid. The painter had a sweet three-year-old daughter and his wife was pregnant. 'We couldn't have another child in China,' he said. 'Child' was a synecdoche.

At forty, I had no love left for ESL. The students, mostly Koreans, were young and sulky and sensed my diffidence. I felt too good for them but I wasn't—I needed their money. Then I got a job offer from a magazine. It was an easy job and the mediocre salary still paid more than I'd ever made.

At the same time, I got into grad school in southern California: five years of funding and I could write a book (this book) to get a PhD. The grad school stipend was crumbs, scraps, chump change, enough for rent and Campbell's and not much else. My decision took all of two minutes: California, here I come. I didn't feel guilty about leaving Williamsburg; Williamsburg had already left me.

After crawling around the site that night, I stepped back through the slashed fence and made my way to the street, sedans from Northside Car Service parked in a line, drivers dozing as they waited for radios to squawk. It was so quiet I could hear a car engine guttering three blocks away. The walk had calmed me but I still wasn't ready to go home. I turned toward Grand Ferry Park, wanting to spend a few more minutes near the water. Even for two-thirty the park was unusually empty: I'd gotten used to seeing Latino couples, random hipsters and Hasidic men there at all hours. I hadn't really understood the park was a Hasid hangout until I walked past a parked car and saw two of them making out, beards tangling and the flash of white shirts (they smoked pot too: the smell was hard to miss). When I'd wriggled under the riverside fence after another New England Petroleum clamber, the black suits had gathered around me. 'You are having an adventure,' one said, beaming. He shook my hand. 'That's right,' I said. We all were getting the same thing from the waterfront.

I took a few steps into the park, hands in my pockets. Nobody sat on the breakwater piled out into the river. I stepped onto the first boulder and hopscotched along. Something moved behind me and I turned to see men rushing toward me. In the background a squad car light spun red. I jumped off the rocks onto the shore. A flashlight burnished my eyes. I took my hands out of my pockets. Very slowly.

What are you doing out here? they said. Two cops, one white, one Asian, both young.

Talking a walk, I said.

They thought about that.

Don't you know? they said. The park closes at sundown.

I knew this in the same way I knew that there was a law about spitting on the sidewalk.

Do you mind if we search you? the Asian cop said.

For what? I said.

You could be carrying a knife or gun, he said. We have to protect ourselves.

Okay, I said, not sure what difference it would have made if I'd said no. A trip to the precinct house, probably.

They patted me down. No shiv, no brass knuckles, no Glock.

I like your jacket, the white cop said. It was a black leather biker jacket. He was right to like it.

They led me to the squad car, where they entered my name and address into a computer (high tech had come to the flatfoots). I was more worried than you would expect, as I'd been ticketed on Kent a couple of weeks earlier for having an open beer on the street. Here's to the new Williamsburg. Fortunately, my name didn't come up.

What's this all about? I said.

Sorry about that, the Asian cop said. Just doing our job.

Cops were polite in the new New York. At least to lucid white guys.

I can't believe you're busting me for walking into the park, I said. That never happened before. It's not posted. I've lived here for fifteen years.

I wasn't around back then, the Asian cop said and smiled, abashed but also making fun of me.

I wondered if old Williamsburg cops missed the

rough-and-tumble of the wild Northside, if they missed Kokie's. Even the police force was changing. The cop who'd given me the open-container ticket was black. A black cop on the Northside? Yet in the old days, if they rolled on you with an open container, they wouldn't write the ticket. The new boundaries were drawing tight.

It's worse than the Giuliani days, I said. You can't walk around without getting harassed.

I don't know anything about Giuliani, the Asian cop said. I'm twenty-five.

That stung. To the cop I was a grumpy middle-aged man, a relic yearning for a place that didn't exist. My Williamsburg didn't matter to him. He had a job to do in the here and now, Williamsburg present. I was a ghost of Williamsburg past, one who was about to be handed a summons. Old age had made me polite and cautious: I waited until I walked around the corner before I tossed the summons in a garbage can. Good luck trying to arrest me on a bench warrant from three thousand miles away.

Acknowledgments

To my mentor, Barry Siegel, for his insights and generosity. To Patricia Pierson for her patience and perspicacity. To the English and Comparative Literature departments at UCI, in particular professors Brook Thomas, Richard Godden, Amy Wilentz, Ackbar Abbas, and Raymond Szalay for his lessons on the historical hipster. To professors Elfie Raymond and Danny Kaiser at Sarah Lawrence College, who insisted I had a future. To Nadia Lesy (hey Boo). To my agent, Scott Waxman, and the folks at FSG. I'd especially like to thank Paul Elie, without whose belief this book would not exist. To all the friends who have shared their memories—Frank Versace, Esther Bell, Chris Miskiewicz, Napoleon, Drew Lichtenstein, Nick Salek, Josh Wick, Sara Gillingham, Wendy Klein, Stephan Drewes, Alexis Sottile, Aaron Aites, Brooke Berman, Brian Kelly, Keith Nelson, Jesselyn Dullea, Anne Widegren and Zach Sebastian. To the clubhouse boys: Phil,

Ali and Tom. To Greg McClure for having my back during some very rough months.

Finally, I'd like to say thank you and farewell to Gerard A. Smith. His departure left the world a darker place. He is missed.